ARE YOU READY FOR THE CHALLENGE TO EXPERIENCE COURAGEOUS FAITH IN YOUR LIFE?

A catalogue record for this work is available from the National Library of Australia

Abrahams, Lynn (author)
Unleashing Courageous Faith: How God took an ordinary girl to live an extraordinary life of faith.
ISBN 978-1-922722-63-8
Christian Living

Typeset Font 11/16

Cover photo by Amy Brunton and Dove image: Colourbox.com/Aleksandra Sabelskaya
Cover and book design by Green Hill Publishing

UNLEASHING *Courageous* FAITH

How God took an ordinary girl to live an extraordinary life of faith.

LYNN ABRAHAMS

Your faith will rise

I met Lynn 12 years ago while serving at church. It was at that first encounter that I immediately knew she was the real deal. She oozed encouragement. Over the next several years, I saw her live the faith walk, not just the faith talk. This book captures Lynn's real life, the highs and the lows, and through her incredible story we see a woman who has held on to God and His Word. We see how her real faith in Jesus has kept her safe and secure. While reading it, I was filled with faith and expectancy in every chapter. Her life's message will make you believe that nothing is impossible for God.

Ps Nina Elmendorp, Senior Pastor, Emerge Church Warner

A compelling message

It is not often that we come across a writer who can so effectively take us into their heart, their family and their relationship with God. In this book, we experience a writer who makes us feel like a valued friend. True spiritual and human intimacy comes from sharing in such humble and gracious ways, ways that capture the very essence of our relationship with God as well as our understanding of grief and loss. In Lynn' book, the true tenacity that comes from our faith is graciously emphasised. This amazing lady captures these concepts in this very easy to read book that walks us through a powerful journey with an appropriately compelling message.

Dr. Rick Sapsford MBBS MGPP FRACGP, Practice Principal

You will be challenged

Lynn's story is an incredible collection of testimonies of God's faithfulness and care over a lifetime, told with authenticity and humility. Lynn's testimonies keep your focus on our 'great and mighty God' and tell her readers that we too can walk through our own circumstances – even the most challenging ones – with the same sense of awe, delight, gratitude and expectant faith in Jesus as she has done herself, by His grace. As you read this book, be prepared to have your faith stirred and your love for Jesus fanned into a flame – and may the Holy Spirit minister to you through these pages as he did me!

Yasmin Henry BMus/Bed, Power to Change, Campus Missionary, University of Queensland

Dedication

To my precious and treasured grandchildren who I love, value and adore so much

- Alexander, Amy,
- Cody, Sierra,
- Charlize, Brianna,
- Ellie and Tyler,
- and the generations to come

You have all been an inspiration for me writing this book — I want you to know our God is able to meet your every need, powerfully and faithfully

"Not one promise from God is empty of power.
Nothing is impossible with God!"
Luke 1-37 (TPT)

About the Author

I was born in Sydney, Australia, and grew up as an unassuming girl who enjoyed the gift of Christian parents and a home that was filled with love and the teachings of our wonderful God. At a very young age, I remember choosing to love and trust God no matter what my future held. "Daddy God," I prayed, "I'm going to truly believe your promises even if I don't understand the path that I will walk."

Throughout my life, I had encountered adversity in many ways, but I knew God was faithful, prayer is powerful, and His promises were true.

Daily, I chose not to give the evil one an inkling that he could win in my circumstances. Did I fail at times? Absolutely, but God would lovingly remind me I was His girl, chosen and set apart for His purposes, and with that assurance, I trusted Him implicitly.

I believe the opportunity of living in Indonesia helped catapult me into the knowledge that the tangible presence of God and His power was continually with me. It helped me understand that speaking out God's word was a powerful weapon that we all too often underestimate as we live in a western society.

What an honour it was for God to count my husband Garry and myself worthy and trustworthy enough to guide the lives of so many young people worldwide even at the age we were. This was an honour beyond what I had ever dreamed possible, that we would see blessings and miracles unleashed over those 14 years that are embedded in my heart forever.

What a privilege it has been to lead Life Groups for so many years in Dubbo, Alstonville, Jakarta, Sydney and now Brisbane. It is an unspeakable joy to share as we study God's word, encourage all to love, exhort and support one another as we go through life together, and continually see the mighty power of God at work.

Intercessory prayer has always been my passion even at a young age. Seeing lives changed, healed and restored, and the broken raised from the ashes has been worth every early morning and late night of intercession. God took the prayers prayed and allowed the miraculous to occur.

Moving to Brisbane where I now live and losing Garry who was my earthly rock has been my greatest challenge. I loved this man as most days were like a date knowing I was his princess. No longer being married, God has been my everything. When the tears flowed, He held me close allowing me to experience His heartbeat along with the knowledge that He would never leave me or forsake me.

I am praying that as you read this book, your faith will rise. Even if it is only the size of a mustard seed, you can move mountains. I have learned much of the power of God in all my challenges, condensed in this book, and many more that are in the storehouse of my memories.

Throughout my life, I loved visualising the evil one shuddering and cringing when I stood firm, even at times when everything seemed insurmountable. God gave me everything I needed to stand resolute in the battle. Satan slinks away when he sees Christians speaking out with the authority that is already ours in the name of Jesus.

At the very moment I called out to you, you answered me! You strengthened me deep within my soul and breathed fresh courage into me.
Psalms 138-3

Special Thanks

I want to thank my wonderful God who has walked beside me throughout all that I have experienced in life. Without Him and all that He has given me, I could never have walked this path of faith, experienced His peace and known His power and victory in every situation.

Even though my treasured Garry is now enjoying heaven with his Lord and Saviour whom he loved, through all the events described in this book, he was my earthly rock. He spoke not a word of criticism, whatever the circumstance, only those of encouragement. Garry, there is no one like you. I was blessed to have had you by my side.

I could never have written this book without the constant help of my beautiful daughter, Kylie. You were there to help, teaching me what was needed on the computer. This book would not have become a reality without your loving encouragement and inspiration as you cheered me on to its completion.

Thank you to my children, Kylie, Darren and Peter, who humbly allowed me the privilege of sharing how God was present in various situations you experienced, resulting in His glory being displayed. In each difficulty, the mighty power of God was unleashed as I stood in faith for you.

Peter, you exhorted and encouraged me with the gift of faith that you said I had been given. Darren wrote the heartfelt foreword of this book. I say thank you to my amazing boys.

I also acknowledge Wayne, Kristy and Lisa, my valued son and daughters-in-law, who stood in support alongside my children and myself, giving love and encouragement in the latter parts of this book.

Thank you, Amy Brunton, my granddaughter who produced the beautiful cover photo for this book. Amy's amazing gift has captured what this book unleashes.

Thank you to the many I have mentioned, who also allowed me the privilege to write of the mighty power of God at work. Each difficulty allowed my faith to grow as I trusted in an ever-faithful God.

Shirley Mead and Janette Meulen, I value the time spent reading and giving much needed advice and edits. You will never know how much your time spent has meant to me.

Kristy Everett, Julie Tasker, Lisa Snowley and Dayna Carfora, your input as I wrote this book was invaluable.

There are too many to name, but thanks to all who came to me after reading the first two chapters which I completed on the tenth anniversary of Garry being taken to heaven. Each came asking when my book would be complete, many with tears in their eyes as they were deeply moved by the power of God. I appreciate your words of love and encouragement.

Contents

Foreword 1
Setting the Scene 7
From crumbs to a banquet 21
The fire rages but God is present 27
The power of praise saves our baby boy 35
A miracle and a visiting angel 49
God, you give me the giggles 59
Our God will use the unexpected 71
My dad saw pink flowers 85
The impossible becomes a reality 95
Dr. Breezy and his disbelief 105
God's speciality is to use ordinary people 115
I am trusting You without understanding 127
Satan is powerless when we know who we are in Christ 139
No foothold for you Satan 151
Will you dare to take up the challenge? 157
Heroes God uses to deepen my faith 163

Foreword

Darren Abrahams

What is it that inspires you? The victorious conquest of a world class athlete, What the rags to riches story of an overlooked entrepreneur, or maybe the "never say die" attitude of the unlikely hero facing all odds.

My mum is one of my inspirations, a humble giant and amazing storyteller whose passion for her Jesus brings life to the broken and elevates the steadfast.

Maybe you are sceptical of motivational tales because there is little connection with the author. If so, come sit alongside someone whom you will get to know and love, and enjoy the warm fire of this comfortable embrace.

I can categorically vouch for the authenticity of these revelations as I am honoured to have had a front row seat in watching this faith-filled stance materialise through Godly example.

My parents forever aligned their passionate mission to encourage and inspire those whom God brought them to feed, love and empower. Therefore, these authentic truths have been lived and documented for you.

But do not just sit as a spectator to these testimonies of God's goodness – as written in the book of Acts.

Now I am certain that God treats all people like.
God is pleased with everyone who worships him and does right, no matter what nation they come from.
Acts 10:34-35 (CEV)

What God has achieved in and through this incredible duo, He also has in His heart to accomplish in and through you.

So, as you read these encouraging chapters, allow yourself to be touched by the Father's heart and join in this great journey powered by the Holy Spirit – celebrating life's peaks and valleys for the glory of Jesus' name.

Setting the Scene

Jesus, my greatest friend, my everything

Don't measure the size of the mountain;
Talk to the one who can move it.
Max Lucado [emphasis mine]

I laugh to myself, even out loud, at the myriad of notes I have written on bits of paper that are scattered around my bedroom floor, beside my bed, in the study. There are also thoughts scribbled on pages in various books which I now cannot find, others which were thrown out in the trash by mistake as I cleaned up. They all share the numerous answers to prayer that I have experienced and witnessed in my life, and I do not want to forget any one of them. I want to share with the world that MY GOD IS SO GOOD.

There have been so many miraculous God-answered prayers, all begging me to shout from the rooftops to those who pass by that my God is over and above all things as I have said to myself and to others so many times:

Now to him who is able to do immeasurably
more than all we ask or imagine…
Ephesians 3:20

I so want to put it out on social media, send a text, share it enthusiastically with my family and friends any way that I can, just letting the world know that Jesus is my everything and can do all things.

He is my greatest and most treasured friend, my confidant. He has become my husband. He dances with me, listens as I walk through my house sharing my innermost thoughts, holds me and wipes my tears away when I cry in those sad, dark, lonely times. He laughs with me when I am silly and no one else is around and encourages me as I sing out loud wishing I had the voice of an angel. He rides in the car with me, but also has His arms outstretched to welcome me home, saying, "Lynn, I've been waiting for you." He comes to coffee and dinner when no-one else is sitting opposite, and literally tells me where things are when I have lost something and cannot remember where I have left it. He loves me with a passion and delights in me as if I am His prized possession, as I read in *Isaiah 49:16: "See, I have engraved you on the palms of my hands; …."*

You may say, "Lynn, I've never experienced this kind of intimacy that I so desire.". As you read this book, I pray you will come to know this inexplicable love, which is so amazing and comes in so many diverse ways. My awesome God has used a variety of people and ways to show me His love: His arms giving hugs and touch; His heart sharing words of love and valuable encouragement; His feet bringing tangible unexpected gifts to my door, all through beautiful caring people.

I have prayed since I was a teenager, "Daddy God, give me eyes to see everything You do, as I don't want to miss the most minuscule thing."

Have I seen everything? I know I have missed so much, and at times I have called out like the great King David, 'Where are You?" But what I have seen and read has given me a heart to love Him passionately through all that I have experienced.

Over the years, as I read His Word, I have learned to keep trusting with child-like faith (even in those times when answers seem to allude me), and I have learned to accept unquestioningly His overall master plan.

My mum wrote a verse in the beautiful white leather zippered Bible that she and Dad gave me for Christmas when I was ten years old. I treasured this so much as I knew they did not have the money to purchase such a beautiful gift. This verse has been so significant and powerful throughout my whole life:

Trust in the LORD with all your heart and lean not on your own understanding; in all your ways submit to Him and He will make your paths straight.
Proverbs 3:5–6

I love to personalise this verse by saying — Trust in the Lord with all your heart Lynn. Lean not on what you think may happen, but in all your ways acknowledge that your God, whom you love and adore, will literally guide your every step.

This verse has become a blueprint in my heart, mind and spirit, and has sprung to life in LED lights when decisions have needed to be made or in stressful circumstances.

When I needed wisdom, this verse continually came flooding back with such intensity that I could literally sense the Holy Spirit in the form of a person whispering in my ear. Oh, the power that is in God's word, and the peace it brings.

- I remember, whilst living at Alstonville, the fear I felt standing at the top of our internal stairs which led to the garage, clutching a sharp bladed kitchen knife in my hand. Our children were asleep, and Garry was on a business trip. I was sure I heard voices and movement in our garage. I thought of this verse in Proverbs and God's promises in the Psalms that He was my shield and my fortress, and He would always be with me. I put the knife back and literally took the hand of Jesus.
- Peter (nine years) and I were alone with our house staff in our huge home whilst living in Jakarta. An Indonesian stranger came to our gate in anger, aggressively demanding he be allowed in. This verse that my mum taught me came flooding into my spirit. I will guide you, Lynn; I'm your protector.

- Garry and I didn't experience fear, but certainly trepidation in Jakarta and Sydney, when, in our mid-forties, we were asked to lead sizeable youth groups. Who at our age is asked to do this work? Moses was older, came the voice of the Holy Spirit. In a later chapter will share the power that God chose to release due to our obedience.
- I watched my treasured husband suffer from an aggressive and rare form of leukaemia as the ugly and horrendous effects of chemotherapy took hold. God's tenderness, compassion and love for me were tangibly unleashed. Tears flowed and sadness gripped my heart, but His faithfulness and closeness were precious and unmistakable when I clung to Him as Garry was taken to his heavenly home.
- What! Spit and use the saliva on my dad's eyes and pray for healing. This was the nudge I heard from the Holy Spirit while reading Smith Wigglesworth's book on faith when I was visiting my blind father, the humbling and amazing outcome I will share in a later chapter.
- When the Holy Spirit asked me to invite a large family for lunch and there was virtually no food in our pantry, I remembered the saying, '*Do it afraid*', that was what I felt drawn to do. Experiencing the same miracles that are written in the Bible added to a walk of faith that was to unfold many times over in the years to come.

To me, God is so real. I wanted to leave a legacy to my children, grand-children and the generations to come, hence the reason I have put pen to paper. This book is also for friends and those who desire to be encouraged by an amazing God. What He has done for me, He can do for all who read.

He will satisfy each and every desire and need if we allow Him. He loves to hold us unconditionally especially when the world says we are of no value and we have allowed the pain of these words to take root in our hearts. He is always there to comfort us when we cry, I hurt so much.

We can see Him take front row position cheering us on so enthusiastically when we need encouragement. He is our everything!

Throughout my life, I believe God has given me the opportunity to choose to live a life of faith. Has it been easy? Not in any way, but it has certainly encouraged me to lean on Him relentlessly, not looking to the right or the left, but to trust Him wholeheartedly. Many great men and women in the Bible are my heroes and I have learnt much from them. What I have written is my story as I have read theirs.

I want to encourage you to look at what God places in your heart, the gifts he offers to you as you walk out your incredible journey with Him. Whatever your path, He promises to be all you need. He will faithfully enable you to go wherever your path leads.

In 1 Corinthians 12:8-10, Paul shares the gifts given which are wisdom, knowledge, faith, healing, miraculous powers and prophecy, distinguishing between spirits, speaking in different kinds of tongues, and interpretations of tongues, along with many others in various passages in God's word.

When He gives His gift to you, He will empower you through the mighty Holy Spirit, He has already given us the fruit of the Spirit so we can live and be like Him. How rich we are!

I love this verse penned by the song writer, Andre Crouch, which I have sung (never in public) but a million times over and know to be so true.

**"Through it all, through it all, I've learned to trust in Jesus.
I've learned to trust in God.
Through it all, through it all, I've learned to depend
upon His Word."[1]**

My absolute desire and prayer is that as you read these pages and what I have shared, you will allow yourself to grow beyond where you are now, to journey and aspire to reach another dimension in your walk with Jesus, believing that—

For nothing is impossible with God.
Luke 1:37

• • • • • • •

I want to begin this book by sharing the greatest decision I have ever chosen to make, that is, to ask Jesus to be my Lord and Saviour.

This is a choice that I have never regretted throughout my entire life and never at any time have I felt to turn away from what was a watershed experience at such an early age.

This most precious encounter is still as vivid to me today as the day it happened so many years ago, as a very young and shy, eight-year-old girl. There is no doubt that this encounter has been pivotal in every decision I have made and will continue to make.

It began like this: My dad and mum took my sister, Colleen, and myself to Kandos, a small town close to Cowra in country New South Wales, to visit some of their distant cousins. The night we arrived at their place; we were taken to what was the last day of a week-long mission at the little Cowra Baptist Church which they attended.

I cannot remember the name of the fiery evangelist or what he even spoke about that Saturday night, but what I do remember was the altar call he made at the conclusion of the service.

"We have had a very successful crusade over this past week, and many of you have come to know Jesus as your Lord and Saviour. If this has been your experience, could you please stand." People in different parts of the little church with its hard, straight-backed wooden pews stood to their feet. Again, his loud, robust voice boomed out, and as an eight-year-old, I found it quite scary!

He went on to say, "I would like all at this meeting who have already made this decision for Jesus to join those already standing."

At those words, my dad, mum and sister, and the people we were staying with all stood up quickly.

I was very aware that I was the only one in my row who was still seated, and one of the very few in this country church not standing. The preacher continued, "Now, for those of you who are still sitting, would you like to make Jesus your Lord and Saviour?" Out of absolute embarrassment, I jumped to my feet, not wanting to be the only person left sitting. This was my experience of becoming a Christian.

I would like to say that the Holy Spirit truly convicted me of my sin, or I felt the amazing presence of God working in my life, or as in lyrics of the beautiful song sang at each Billy Graham Crusade, 'All to Jesus I surrender, all to Him I freely give', none of these transpired that night I gave my life resolutely to Jesus.

Even though I was young and it was out of embarrassment, it did not seem to matter to God because what I do know is that I stood up to say, "I will make Jesus Lord and Saviour of my life," and nothing that I have encountered since that night has ever detracted from the decision I made, as unorthodox as it may have been.

I went back to Sydney, overflowing with a new power that I had never experienced and I wanted everyone to know that I was now a Christian.

This was the beginning of my Christian life, where I had been impregnated with the fruit and power of the Holy Spirit and a burning desire to live a life sold to Him, holding nothing back.

Throughout my life, there certainly have been times of amazing joy, relentless storms and desert experiences when I needed to stand and keep standing in faith, not knowing when the answers would come. What is written by Paul, who was called to be an apostle, has often been my story.

We are hard pressed on every side, but not crushed; perplexed,
but not in despair; persecuted, but not abandoned;
struck down, but not destroyed.
2 Corinthians 4:8–9

As Paul recorded some in his writings, these are a couple of my experiences:

- My treasured God-given husband, Garry, was called to his heavenly home, even though we together stood resolutely every day on God's faithful Word, believing, praying, praising, expecting healing to come, and believing death was not an option.
- Six days before Christmas 2008 while in hospital, a hideous virus attacked his sinuses, and we were faced with the news that Garry was to lose half his face due to the severity of this virus, which was making its way to his brain, consuming everything in its path.

- Our son Peter, at 18 months, was inflicted by a side-effect of German measles, losing all the platelets in his blood and bleeding from various parts of his body. Due to the intensity of this disease, the doctors were unable to give us any guarantees that he would live.
- Again, at ten years, Peter was cursed after one of our house staff in Jakarta was dismissed. With the money received, this man went to a witch doctor for a curse to be placed on our son. Unbeknownst to us, this was a regular practice if staff had their services terminated. This powerful, hideous, relentless spirit of fear instantly came upon Peter and literally crippled and paralysed our son over the following four years.
- Kylie, our beautiful daughter, was led into the club scene and drinking by the young people in the church she was attending while we were still living in Jakarta. I fought in the heavenlies, saying, "Satan, you will never have my daughter," and to see the awesome and miraculous answer that unfolded.
- Receiving a phone call from my son, Darren, sharing the news that it seemed impossible that his beautiful wife would fall pregnant. Choosing to believe that nothing was hopeless or unattainable for God, my faith rose to a new level. I remember screaming out, "God is greater than any negative prognosis, my God is able!"

These I will unfold in later chapters, as I detail how I experienced the incredible prevailing work of God, as prayer, praise and faith were unleashed to a God who is able. I need to say with everything that is within me, that through every experience nothing has ever caused me to re-think the life-long commitment I made that night when I was eight years old in that little country church. Jesus was and still is my Lord and Saviour; God is my ever-faithful, ever-loving, ever-truthful mighty God.

In abundance or hardship, there always comes the inexpressible knowledge of knowing Jesus is my everything. He gives me an unspeakable joy. It is like a deep well that releases joy like an irrepressible fountain. Just ask Cody my grandson, as I would dance with him around his kitchen when he was young whilst singing, "I've got the joy joy joy joy down in my heart". This is a very old song that I learned when I was his age but still so relevant.

The night I became a Christian, there were no bells and whistles or warm fuzzy feelings. No spirit-filled worship song nor prophetic words given, only the absolute knowledge that I had become a daughter of the King, with the resolute knowledge of the course I had chosen. Nothing was ever going to change the greatest decision of my life.

I want the following chapters in this book to encourage you, excite you, challenge you and take you to another dimension of faith. I will share the incredible answers to my heartfelt prayers and challenge you with the gifts that have been given to you.

I have learned not to expect God to answer my way, because when I think I know what is best, it is as if He jumps out of the box and says, "Lynn, did I surprise you with my answer?" He is so creative, and He makes me smile and even laugh. I love Him so much and wish I could hug Him just because of who He is, and what He means to me as I stand in awe of His greatness.

I trust him implicitly. I want to encourage you, no matter what the circumstance, to trust Him, not looking to the right or the left, but directly into the eyes of the One who created you. He is good, He is faithful, and He is our everything.

The following verses are those I printed out and tenaciously held as I prayed. I have often laughed, thinking they are now so squashed, and no one else can ever use them again.

The One who calls you is faithful, and He will do it.
1 Thessalonians 5:24

Nothing is impossible for God!"
Luke 1:37 (CEV)

Let us not become weary in doing good, for at the proper time we will reap a harvest if we do not give up.
Galatians 6:9

Now to Him who is able to do immeasurably more than all we ask or imagine, according to his power that is at work within us,
Ephesians 3:20

My prayer is: faith will rise and you be challenged as you read my journey. You will be inspired and excited to reach greater heights using the gifts God has placed in your hands.

Expect an unleashing of all that God has for you to experience, as you trust unreservedly His mighty power.

From crumbs to a banquet

We live by faith, not by sight.
2 Corinthians 5:7

Garry and I had not been attending Lugarno Baptist Church for long when we started to feel the love and acceptance from the beautiful Christian families.

We were in our twenties with two babies, Kylie and Darren, which made it easier to integrate, as their cuteness and baby antics helped endear us to others. Above all, our greatest desire as we prayerfully searched for a godly church was to find a place where we could grow in our Christian walk and ultimately minister.

With a twinkle in God's eye, I can even now see Him smiling as He thought, "They won't be waiting long for their desire for growth to be tried and tested."

It was one Saturday afternoon when the Holy Spirit spoke so clearly to me, "Ask the Frazer family around for lunch tomorrow." We loved this family, but I immediately thought, they have four teenage children, and the shops are now closed. We have virtually no food in the cupboard. In fact, at the time, we were living from week to week on Garry's wage, so we had no extra money. I knew I had heard distinctly from God, so I asked, "Lord, what will we eat?"

"Open your cupboard," came the reply. A little shaken, I opened my cupboard. Yes, there was one large tin of salmon, some potatoes and herbs, but will this be enough I questioned, and what about dessert?

"Open your cupboard again." A mixture of apprehension and excitement welled up as my eyes were drawn to the flour and eggs. "God, are You saying, herbed salmon patties and vegetables with pancakes and ice-cream for dessert?"

"Yes! A perfect meal for any family," I felt God saying in my Spirit.

How could I make these insufficient groceries spread over six adults plus our family? I cannot begin to tell you what I was feeling. Such a simple, bland and small meal we would be providing. Garry and I held our hands together and prayed that this family would experience a love and joy that would be mixed with these meagre ingredients, as some uneasiness crept in.

Garry and I loved God fervently, but this was another level that we were embarking on. With our eyes firmly fixed on Him, I made the phone call inviting this beautiful family for lunch. Even though we did it in what I would call 'afraid faith', the answer to our invitation was met with great eagerness. "Yes, we would love to come."

Any mum who has just invited a large family for a meal with what I had in my hands would be calculating. If I were to make the patties tiny, I may be able to give them two each and one for Garry and myself.

"I'm your provider Lynn; all I want is your obedience and trust, and I will do the rest."

The next morning, as we arrived at church, the display of enthusiasm and warm affection from this welcoming and kind family towards us was overwhelming. This made me somewhat embarrassed as I thought of the mediocre tiny patties and simple pancakes that lay waiting at home. Mixed with these emotions, came the joy of the Spirit saying, "Thank you for your willingness; that's all I want."

With the table set and food heating, Kylie and Darren sensed something was about to happen as they clapped their chubby little hands with joy while we waited for the doorbell to ring. We both sensed our time together would be God-honouring in every way, and believed that what we lacked in food, we would fill with love.

At last, the chatter of voices drifted from our driveway and we opened the door.

As this family of six stood at our door, our eyes took some time to focus and comprehend what was before us – 12 arms laden with abundance! There were chickens, salads, desserts and a myriad of delectable foods, enough to feed the five thousand, as is shared in God's word.

Still, I know my little patties shone that day amongst the smorgasbord of food at lunch, and I think I could even hear them singing, "How Great Is Our God."

We did not have to buy food that week because of the miracle that Garry and I witnessed. Yes, what was given filled our bodies but what we experienced filled and overflowed our spiritual reservoir. The floodgates were opened to another level of God and all that He was showing and teaching us.

Our lunch together that day was certainly a celebration as we shared and encouraged each other with all that God was doing.

What Garry and I experienced that Sunday afternoon was nothing less than God's faithfulness. It has been etched in my mind and stamped on my heart forever. This was one of the steppingstones in my walk of faith.

• • • • • • •

The Holy Spirit whispered ever so clearly, "Garry and Lynn, due to your joyful obedience, and at the same time of doing it afraid, you will never forget what I have done today, and I will place in you both a faith that will be unleashed many times over."

The fire rages but God is present

Rejoice in the LORD always. I will say it again: Rejoice!
Philippians 4:4

People often mistake what this verse is saying, thinking they are to rejoice in their trial, but that is not what Paul is writing. This great Apostle is saying to rejoice in the Lord during our trials. We as Christians have this capacity, due to joy being a fruit of the Spirit, and we carry it continually. It is a deep abiding joy.

How faithful God has always been through every battle we have faced. How assured we can be because of His promise of never leaving us or forsaking us, even if we do not always feel this closeness.

Garry was working for a high profile corporate Australian company, and as part of his goal to climb the corporate ladder, he needed country experience. He was successful in his application for a country posting to Dubbo, a city in the Orana Region of New South Wales. This experience was imperative if you were aiming to be in a managerial position in the company. Very quickly he became aware that his new boss, I will call him KI, who was based in Sydney and oversaw all branch managers, had a disdain for Christians. Garry was not one who spoke out loudly about his Christian faith but his whole demeanour radiated Jesus. His work ethic, his respect for clients and colleagues, the jokes he shared, the honour he gave to those in authority: without saying a word, Jesus in all His glory shone through.

As the days, weeks and months passed, this disdain from his boss escalated, and his behaviour towards Garry would have been, in today's terminology, tantamount to workplace bullying. This man would only give instructions through his secretary, not wanting to speak face-to-face or by phone to Garry. When it was imperative to speak, he would address Garry in derogatory terms, such as 'Sonny'. At managerial meetings and seminars, the humiliation became greater. In one of the Financial Distribution meetings, in front of all Garry's colleagues, he sarcastically said, "Why give Abrahams any money for his branch? He will more than likely spend it on the church bus." Humiliating comments soon became normal as KI sought to belittle Garry in the eyes of all.

Garry was revered by the executive staff, but no one had what it took to stand up to this person of influence.

The fire became hotter as the flames leapt around Garry. To those who are reading this chapter, I want to say, no matter what, God is aware of what we are experiencing, be it our health, reputation, finances, hurts or circumstances we just do not understand.

These are the times when we have the privilege to sprint as fast as we can, not stopping but running to our God so He can show us what artillery we have at our disposal, and then to use what He has given, believing His weapons are anointed and full of power.

In this battle, we chose the weapons from our armoury that we believed would bring victory:

The weapons we fight with are not the weapons of the world. On the contrary, they have divine power to demolish strongholds.
2 Corinthians 10:4

Each morning, our family prayed. Yes, even though Kylie and Darren were young, we were not going to let them miss out on seeing the power that was about to unfold. I wanted them to see our God at work through what they prayed for their daddy.

We sat on our lounge-room floor together holding hands and prayed. We asked for strength so Garry could endure the fight that Satan was engineering, and that the fruit of the Spirit would shine through him for the world to see as the weapons given were mighty for the trials we faced. We prayed, and believed that in the fire, Garry would stand and not be burned. We also prayed for a mighty blessing for KI, that through my husband, he would see and know Jesus, and that he would come to honour and respect Garry as an equal.

As Garry left for work each day, wrapped in authority and power that is ours, he would say how rich he was to have a family who encouraged and exhorted him.

Consider it pure joy, my brothers and sisters, whenever you face trials of many kinds, because you know that the testing of your faith produces perseverance. Let your perseverance finish its work so that you may be mature and complete, not lacking anything.

James 1:2–4

Many people would prefer that this verse is not in the Bible, but it is there for our growth, and for us to perfect our faith and trust. It is not a superficial joy, but a deep abiding joy of knowing that Jesus is with us in each trial we encounter.

Our prayers were not answered by Garry's boss showing kindness and the barrage of humiliation coming to an end. *God chose a greater way*, one that this man would never forget. KI became very sick as cancer infiltrated his body and he was hospitalised.

When we surrender to Him, the love of God permeates our hearts to strengthen us in our spirit so we are able to act in a way that the world would think is totally crazy. With God's love flowing through every fibre of Garry's being, he went to visit his boss.

The utter surprise that this man demonstrated as Garry walked into his hospital room was palpable. "Why would you come to visit me with the way I have relentlessly scorned and humiliated you? None of those whom I would call my colleagues and friends at our office have come, but here you are!"

Tears welled up in his eyes, and it was clear that his heart softened. Garry treated him with the love that Jesus would, sharing what the Holy Spirit gave to him, not preaching to or at him, just loving him. KI later died. Did he come to know Jesus? Only God knows the answer, but as he stood in front of God, he could never say I did not ever encounter Jesus because Garry was Jesus to him that day.

'For I was hungry and you gave me something to eat, I was thirsty and you gave me something to drink, I was a stranger and you invited me in, I needed clothes and you clothed me, I was sick and you looked after me, I was in prison and you came to visit me." Then the righteous will answer him, "Lord, when did we see you hungry and feed you, or thirsty and give you something to drink? When did we see you a stranger and invite you in, or needing clothes and clothe you? When did we see you sick or in prison and go to visit you?" The King will reply, "Truly I tell you, whatever you did for one of the least of these brothers and sisters of mine, you did for me."

Matthew 25:35–40

We do not always see the outcome of our prayer. We only need to go to Hebrews Chapter 11 to see that none of these mighty men and women, even with their faith, ever got to see the fulfilment of what they believed. These mighty saints continued to stand until God took them home but all they believed ultimately came to be.

Sometime after KI died, I was in the city, entering a lift in a Myer store. I saw a man who had worked some time back at this same place of employment which I had also worked. As we chatted, the man said, "Lynn, I am not sure why I am telling you this, but I know you would be very aware of what KI thought of Garry. However, there is something that you may not know. Just days before he was diagnosed with cancer, he shared these words. 'I may not agree or even like Christians, in fact I hate each one of them, but I believe I need to honour and respect Garry, no matter how I feel.'" I thanked Kevin for sharing as I exited the lift. Kevin had used the words "honour and respect", the same words we prayed each morning, kneeling together as a family. I was so excited God had answered our prayers. I could not wait to tell Garry, Kylie, and Darren, and in my classic style, I burst out singing that old hymn, 'To God be the glory, great things he has done!'

We, as a family, never forgot the power that was ours as we prayed unwavering prayers those mornings as the fire in Garry's circumstance burned furiously. What did we choose throughout those months that God had already given to us?

Prayer — Faith — Praise
But we dug deeper into God's reservoir and found
Trust — Rest — Peace

How good God was to show us the latter three as they helped us to not be anxious as the flames grew hot and leapt high, but each one kept Garry from being burned.

• • • • • • •

I encourage you to know what you have been given as a son or daughter of the King. Our weapons come packed with power and go right to the Source as we put our circumstances in the hands of the One who is our answer – not focusing on the crisis but to trust and stand firm, no matter what path we have been given to walk.

The power of praise saves our baby boy

…we capture, like prisoners of war, every thought and insist that it bow in obedience to the Anointed One.
2 Corinthians 10:5 (TPT)

Tears cascaded down our faces as Garry and I knelt in each other's arms beside our little two-year old son's bed. We entrusted him into the hands of Jesus, not knowing if that meant he would live or die from the sickness that had permeated his little body.

Peter was young, inquisitive, and full of life, a bundle of joy with his blonde hair that bounced whenever he ran, dimples so deep I whispered that girls would one day want to fill them with kisses. To this, he would cover them with his chubby little hands and say, "No, mummy." His infectious smile won the hearts of all who met him. This treasured God-given little man was truly a gift to us.

Our children, Kylie and Darren, had now recovered from German measles and Peter was almost back to normal or so we thought. Instead of going to church, we chose to take a drive to Ballina Beach to build sandcastles, paddle and splash in the water as therapy after having been at home those past weeks. We believed the salty air would bring added healing.

"Garry, stop the car!!" I called out in alarm. Peter had just yawned, and what I saw shocked me. The inside of his mouth was purple. As the car came to a stop, I looked again. His gums were bleeding, throat and tonsils purple, and tiny purple spots dotted his little body. With an anxious motherly tone, I began to speak but Garry finished my sentence, "We need to take him back to the doctors NOW!"

Our family sat in the surgery as Dr. Lemon examined our precious little boy. Then in a voice that was less than encouraging, he said,

"Blood tests will need to be taken but leukaemia may be a possibility. We will need to act fast, but I will know more in a few days."

"No God, Peter is our treasured miracle baby." Those heart-felt words rose as I blurted them out from deep within my being, releasing a myriad of emotions and remembering what had transpired for this little guy to become our God-given gift.

Two years prior, we were on our way for a family holiday. As we pulled away from our home in Dubbo, we took the time, as was our normal practice, to pray, asking God that we would arrive at Nambucca Heads safely, which would be our holiday destination with friends for the ensuing two weeks. We were so excited.

Playing games with our children in the car was always fun as we travelled. There were no iPads or video screens in those days, only small electronic games like Donkey Kong and Oil Panic. These, together with the excitement of catching up with their friends from Sydney, filled those hours of driving.

In a moment of time, a vehicle travelling at high-speed tore through a red light intersection at Gunnedah, and smashed our car with such force our car spun 360 degrees, only to be hit again and again.

As we scrambled, dazed and shaken, from our totally demolished vehicle, we heard sirens coming from all directions. Hugging each other as we sat on the gutter with our children and trying to make sense of all that had just transpired, a police officer said to us, "This is a miracle. Throughout my career, never have I seen a car so badly damaged but with no injuries to those involved. It's as if someone had put their hand over you as a family while your car was being destroyed." There was no need for an ambulance or visit to a doctor. Just arrangements for another vehicle so we could continue to our destination.

It was all so surreal. A major accident, then the following day holidaying and sunbaking on the beach with friends. But this relaxation period was not to last as I became incredibly sick. Thinking the sickness was from the shock of our accident, our friends gave me all kinds of advice, fasting, herbal medicine, all to no avail. The vomiting was relentless.

On our return from holidays, my doctor, said, "Lynn, do you think you may be pregnant?" With a giggle of absolute certainty, I replied, "No, I can't be, I know my body." With a glint in his eye and thinking, I have heard these words many times, he chose to run a test just for his own satisfaction due to the persistence of my sickness.

"Well, Mrs Abrahams, I believe you will need to prepare yourself for many sleepless nights in approximately eight months. You are pregnant!"

I wanted to be excited about this unexpected news, surprising as it was. The persistent sickness was robbing me of the joy I was meant to be sharing with my treasured husband.

On my next visit to the doctor, his words to me were, "Lynn, you can't go on like this. Let me recommend a tablet that I'm sure will help. You can start with three daily and increase to six, if necessary." Little did I know at the time, and neither did the world, of the severe ramifications of this medication called Debendox on the unborn foetus. I took six tablets daily for seven and a half months of my pregnancy, and still the sickness did not abate.

DEBENDOX
(Hansard, 25 July 1984) - UK Parliament
HC Deb 25 July 1984 Vol 64 cc1165-79
Mr. Greville Janner (Leicester, West)[2]

"I am happy to have the opportunity to draw the attention of the House to the general picture on product liability and to the tragedy of Debendox in particular. I ask the Government to assist those members of the public who are already struck

by tragedy in no way of their making, especially those 70 British families whose children have been disabled because of the drug Debendox."

"Nevertheless, the fact is the mothers who took Debendox gave birth to children who were damaged by that morning sickness drug In the United Kingdom the manufacturers Merrell Dow decided to pay nothing to those families, nothing to those children and nothing to provide some solace for those who suffered as a result of taking the drug."

DEBENDOX AND CONGENITAL MALFORMATIONS IN NORTHERN IRELAND
Research Article BMJ[3]

"An investigation was carried out in Northern Ireland into the alleged association between fetal abnormalities and Debendox, an antiemetic drug used in pregnancy."

On 25th of May 1979, Peter Troy Abrahams, truly a gift from God was born with the help of forceps, but he was beautifully and perfectly formed in every way. No foetal malformation, no birth defect and no disability, only a baby that would be used in the future to help grow my faith.

• • • • • • •

Two days later apprehensively we made our way back to the surgery after many hours on our knees in prayer. We trusted as we waited for answers from the blood tests that would confirm the diagnosis of Peter's condition. We sat and listened as Dr Lemon shared. No smiles but instead a look of concern as he uttered the strained and difficult words: “Garry and Lynn, Peter doesn’t have leukemia, but the diagnosis is a severe case of idiopathic thrombocytopenic purpura. At this time there is no medication that we can administer, and his own little body must do the work of healing. I can give you no certainty of a good prognosis. I have spoken to all our doctors in this practice, and no one will give any assurance that Peter will make it through this sickness. Peter really should be in hospital.” Dr. Lemon continued, “He has virtually no platelets, hence all the bruising and bleeding. He will need to have a blood test every day to see what is happening. I have trust and faith in you as parents so I will not admit him but if he collapses, rush him to hospital as fast as you can. Do not spare a moment. Will you give me your word?” Not even Dr. Paul Earner, who was one of our closest friends and a physician at this medical practice, would give us the assurance we wanted to hear.

For the following four months, my heart broke as I took my little man for a blood test every day. Watching the pathologist search for a vein in his little arm already badly bruised so blood could be drawn, tears would well up. As I walked up the path to that dreaded surgery, I would sing little praise songs to Peter so fear would not rise in him or me. To be able to cling to Daddy God was a comfort beyond measure.

One night, Peter lay listless on his bed, with hardly a spot on his little body that was not bruised. Knowing nothing could be done physically, Garry and I laid our hands on him as we knelt beside his bed and prayed.

“God, we don’t know what it would be like to lose our little boy, but we have trusted You all our lives and whatever happens we will still love You. You have given us so much, and blessed us with our adorable Kylie and Darren, and helped us through many difficult circumstances. We now ask that You bring healing to our precious Peter, as we give him to You and thank You for what will be.”

Tears flowed as we kissed him, held each other and whispered, "We will not doubt but enjoy every day as a family, teaching our children to love You and trust You in everything."

What a blessing to have a wonderful man of God as my husband. He was my earthly rock. He always encouraged me to keep my eyes firmly fixed on Jesus. I loved him passionately. As one pastor shared, Garry was the closest to Jesus he had ever met.

Were these months easy, as we waited for Peter's healing? Not in any way, and I came to know what it was to be fraught with thoughts and experience the distress that Satan tried to instil as we chose to tightly hold onto God, whom we knew was aware of everything we were experiencing.

As I trusted and held tenaciously to the peace that God had given us, I also became incredibly aware of voices that would occupy my thought pattern, saying, "Peter is going to die, and there is nothing you can do." These cruel and evil voices would try to dominate my thinking day and night. Becoming tired of their harassment, I allowed these negative words to settle into my sad heart.

At that point, I believe my wonderful God said, "Enough is enough," and spoke clearly and unmistakably to me. "Lynn, the enemy has come to destroy and rob you of the peace that I have imparted. Fight Lynn, fight! It's a spiritual battle and I have given you every resource you will need to stand up and fight."

For our struggle is not against flesh and blood, but against the rulers, against the authorities, against the powers of this dark world and against the spiritual forces of evil in the heavenly realms.

Ephesians 6:12

The Power of Praise

With that conviction, I ran to my sound system and put on tapes of praise (as they were called in those days). I chose continually to have praise music and God's word filling our home, my mind and my spirit. When the voices fought to rise above the praise, I would turn up the volume.

We capture, like prisoners of war, every thought and insist that it bows in obedience to the anointed One.
2 Corinthians 10:5b (TPT)

How empowering it was not to fight alone but visualise all of Heaven's armies fighting with me and for me. Every time a negative thought would come, I would be ready with praise as my weapon. Many times I scurried to that sound system, but I never gave up. I believe we can wear the evil one down if we remain steadfast, until the demons get tired, especially when you remind them Who they are fighting against. They know that they can never win, especially when we fight with God's word and praise, but they will try.

We need to know that we are the victors because of Jesus and what He did on the cross, but they hope we will give in before they do. With the strength that God gives us, we have the fortitude to finish the race strongly. So, in this battle, with my armour in place, I was fighting to win, fighting to see my baby boy healed and whole. I was out to let the demonic force know they were messing with the wrong girl because I knew my authority in Jesus.

And having disarmed the powers and authorities, he made a public spectacle of them, triumphing over them by the cross.
Colossians 2:15

The Battle Was about to be Won

I will never forget that Saturday afternoon. I was on our front patio, Garry was mowing the lawn, Kylie and Darren were riding their bikes in the park opposite, and Peter was asleep, when the ugly persistent voices rose again, "Peter will die, and there is nothing you can do." Immediately I again ran inside and unleashed a celebration of adoration and worship to our awesome God. I believe the village of Alstonville with all three thousand people could have heard my praise ringing out. I returned to the patio and a voice emerged clearly, almost tangibly. Crazy as that sounds, I felt I could have touched it. "Lynn, we are leaving you for a season, but we will be back."

Through Jesus, the battle was won. They gave up. The voices were defeated, their work was taken captive, praise had overcome.

But thanks be to God! He gives us the victory
through our Lord Jesus Christ.
1 Corinthians 15:57

Healing was unleashed. With the bruises fading, we rejoiced and were excited every day. We experienced Peter's body being made whole as the platelets elevated.

The Power of Prayer

Daddy God, I can never thank You enough
for your Church of praying people.

After six months, our miracle baby boy now almost back to full health, I was able to take Peter out. Due to a few bruises still evident, I continued dressing him in long sleeved tops and jeans so it did not appear like I was an abusive mum. On one particular day I believe I experienced a divine appointment that bought so much encouragement. I walked into the Christian Book Shop in Lismore. Whilst making my selection, I saw Peter about to do something mischievous as is normal for a two-year-old. I called out, "Peter Abrahams!" A customer in the shop stopped and asked, "Is this little boy Peter Abrahams who has been very sick?" With a surprised look, I said, "Yes." She then knelt in front of Peter and placed her hands on him. I was unsure if she was going to hug him, pray over him or anoint him. The lady, whom I had never met, said to me, "My husband and I have been traveling for some time up the north coast of New South Wales and Queensland, and every Baptist Church we attended took time to pray for a little Peter Abrahams."

Tears of thankfulness and joy flowed with the realisation that God's people counted our son worthy of their prayer.

As Peter grew, I came to see why the evil one would try to take him, as I have also reflected elsewhere in this book. From a young age, Peter has been a blessing, not only to us as parents, but to many others. Peter continues to be a mighty man of God living powerfully for God's kingdom to this day.

At four years, Peter would take whatever he could from my cupboard: cookies, groceries, teabags, fruit or whatever delighted him. Each week, prior to the Life Group meetings held in our home, our young entrepreneur would set up shop at our front door and sell these items to people as they arrived. Being exceptionally cute with an endearing personality, people naturally purchased these items. He would then put the money into an envelope each Sunday and place it in the offering saying, "Mummy, I want to give this money to the missionaries," never a thought of keeping it for himself. I would laugh as these wonderful people returned the items to me as they left, only to buy them again the following week. Peter also loved to pick up all the leaves that fell in our yard, putting them into bags and then selling them to our neighbours for mulch.

At four years, with his dad's guitar he would sit on the front lawn and busk in his sweet childish voice, again placing all he received into the offering the following Sunday. All the money raised by this little guy, who was healed and set free by the mighty power of our wonderful God as prayer, praise, and faith, were lifted high, would have amounted to hundreds of dollars.

I learned to love, trust and live for God, not only in the good times but when troubles, worries, struggles and uncertainty came, and even in times of not understanding.

Unapologetically, I say—

Our God is over all, our God is above all, our God is more than we can ever think dream or imagine. Our God is trustworthy, dependable, faithful and so much more.

His ways are above ours; our thoughts are no match to His thoughts. Just bathe and rest in His promises as we put on our spiritual blinkers and look into His eyes, saying, I will only trust in You.

Praise paralyses the work of the enemy
Praise brings hope in the midst of the storm
Praise ushers in the presence of God
Praise makes a way for God's power to be unleashed

A miracle and a visiting angel

Have eyes to see every touch of God as a treasured miracle

Stepping from our Qantas flight into Soekarno-Hatta International Airport, Jakarta, Indonesia, the high temperature was oppressive and the air was incredibly humid. After making our way through customs, we were faced with what seemed like a million dark-faced people all scrambling to be the first to carry your bags for a price, to touch you, take your photo, to speak to you in a language you did not understand, but all were ever so friendly.

Garry's employer had placed him on a transfer to Jakarta, believing that he was the best employee to start this new venture. We knew with absolute certainty God had led and prepared us for this assignment, and an excitement was welling up within us. We had left our familiar surroundings in Australia for this new land where we knew no one and were very naïve.

For we are God's handiwork, created in Christ Jesus to do good works, which God prepared in advance for us to do.
Ephesians 2:10

With no travel experience, this buzzing and strange city was certainly intriguing. There were many forms of unusual transportation, people were hanging out the doors of dilapidated orange buses, and every type of cart was piled high with merchandise from household goods, tyres, grass, brooms, live chooks tied by their feet, wings flapping, or other animals. Motorcycles carrying families, often with up to four children aboard, smiled and waved as they passed by. Men, women, and children, some deformed, begging for some of the wealth they thought we had, due to us being white. Everything that stood still or moved seemed to call out – *Welcome to Indonesia, appreciate our culture, people, and lifestyle!* Again, we were assured God had divinely guided us and we were excited and ready for the adventure. As we embraced our new surroundings, there was a peace mixed with joy that came from God himself.

With Garry's official work documents not yet in order, we enjoyed the extravagance of staying in the opulent Hilton Hotel. This was an absolute treat and was to be our home for the following six months. We loved eating at the many and varied restaurants, lapping up the services from staff, swimming in the luxurious pools and revelled in this new experience.

Kylie, Darren and Peter had now settled into Jakarta International School (JIS). It was comical to see them racing through the corridors of the hotel to catch the 6.20am school bus that arrived to pick up the students for a 7.30am school start. Not once was there a complaint as the alarm rang out at 5.30am each morning. Garry was also becoming acclimatised to his new work-place environment which was so vastly different from that of the Australian corporate world.

And then there was me! What do I do all day, with no work or friends and being unable to drive? To say I filled my days differently was an understatement. "God, it's just You and me. What is in store for us today?" This was my prayer each morning as I tried to accustom myself to my days being so diverse. No part time work, washing, ironing, cooking, taking the children to school, or leading a ladies' Bible study, what was I to do? My absolute love of meeting and encouraging a friend over a coffee at my favourite quirky café had been left behind in Australia, and now there were different avenues to explore.

Everything was unfamiliar. In those early days, with the language barrier and not knowing anyone, I felt alone at times. One day, I leant against the wall in my bedroom with thoughts of what I would be doing in Australia meandering through my mind. Miraculously, right at that time a common sparrow flew and settled on the sill – yes, to bring me a message through a familiar and comforting voice: "I haven't forgotten you, Lynn. You are here because I have led you, you are on a divine appointment."

You can buy two sparrows for only a copper coin, yet not even one sparrow falls from its nest without the knowledge of your Father. Aren't you worth much more to God than many sparrows? So don't worry. For your Father cares deeply about even the smallest detail of your life.
Matthew 10:29,31 (TPT)

How humbling, God counted me worthy enough to receive a personal message via a tiny sparrow. How blessed! Yes, how incredibly blessed, knowing I would need that assurance in the days that lay ahead. Whilst staying at the hotel, I started enjoying a welcomed lifestyle of tennis lessons, photography, or lazing around the pool as I sipped on a coke or read a book – all awesome pastimes in this city, a complete departure to what I had known. I also prayed and longed to be involved with ladies who had similar passions to mine. Finding a driver that would suit our family was certainly on the top of my priority list.

Some weeks later, with my newly acquired driver and now able to be out and about, I was on the cusp of a miraculous experience. What was about to unravel was so unforeseen and unpredictable and I was totally unprepared.

Even as I write this, I am in awe, and I can only accept the events that unfolded by faith, believing God was showing me that no matter what lay ahead, He is always enough.

It started out like any other day. Aziz, Garry's Indonesian driver, had driven him to work. Kylie, Darren and Peter had left for school. That afternoon, I was at the beautiful, huge house we had just rented and was stripping it of hidden spiritual objects placed above doors and other places by our house staff when I received an unexpected phone call from Garry. I could barely understand the words he was saying due to his distress. "Come back to the hotel, Lynn, I'm not well."

As fast as we could, Harry drove, his hand pressed continually on the horn which was standard practice for Jakarta. He weaved his way with great precision through the afternoon traffic to the hotel where I found Garry, pale and incredibly sick. I had never seen him this way before. "Harry, how long will it take us to drive to SOS Medika (the medical centre used by the expatriate community)?". In broken English, Harry said, "Mrs Lynn, long long time, many cars, all coming home from work, traffic very big."

With school now finished for the day, as calmly as I could, I asked Kylie, Darren and Peter to stay at the hotel and be close to the phone, we all then helped carry Garry to our Mitsubishi van.

After driving for some time, I looked down at Garry's white, clammy, limp body. He beckoned me to come close, and breathlessly whispered, "Lynn, I don't think I'm going to make it, I can't breathe." With an anxious and raised voice, I asked, "Harry how much further?"

"Still long way many many cars. What do I do, Mrs Lynn?" he uttered frantically.

I knew God did not show us so clearly that we were to come to Indonesia for my treasured Garry to die on the back seat of a car before our work for Him had even begun. I called back to Harry, "You drive as fast as you can, and I'll pray." "*JESUS, I NEED YOU, I NEED YOU.*"

No other words would come out as I held Garry's helpless body in my arms.

"Mrs Lynn, Mrs Lynn! What happened! We are here! What happened? Mrs Lynn!" I looked up and my dark-skinned driver now almost white, was driving through the gates of SOS Medika. At that time, I had no answers to give to my driver.

Was this a miracle? Had we been transported supernaturally? I did not have time to think. All I knew and believed was that we were about to get help for the guy I loved more than life itself.

Doctors rushed to read his blood pressure, listened to his heart-beat, and took blood samples. Tubes and needles were placed anywhere where there was spare skin, and with their grave faces, the Indonesian physicians administered what they thought necessary. Amongst the chaos, the Holy Spirit brought peace and calm as I sat, allowing the flurry of medical staff to do their job, and I prayed. Hours later and now nightfall, Garry seemed calm and was breathing regularly again. At this time, the doctor came to speak to me. "We don't know exactly what happened, but Mr Garry was a very sick man, and the crisis has now passed. You arrived just in time. A moment later would have been too late. Rest is what is needed now. We will allow him to return to the hotel, but he needs to have this medication urgently, with food. If another attack comes, return immediately without waiting," the doctor making it clear I understood the seriousness of the situation. I called the hotel and shared what had been happening with the children. They had been so amazingly patient. I told them we were now returning, as praise overflowed from every fibre of my being.

On arriving at the hotel, I immediately called room service so Garry could have the medication prescribed. The bell to our hotel apartment rang and I rushed to the door. Holding a tray, the man who appeared to be delivering room service, stood in the open doorway. He spoke with an authority that stunned me. "Mrs Lynn, you are not to be afraid, you are not to be concerned, Mr. Garry will be healed." What was I hearing, what were these words, who is this man? Does someone delivering room service speak like this? He strode in, placed the tray of food on the table, turned and walked directly to the doorway of the room where Garry was laying. Again he spoke with the same authority, this time stretching his hand towards Garry said, "You are not to be afraid. You are not to be concerned. Mr. Garry you will be healed."

With that, he left, closing the door behind him. I quickly turned to our children, almost speechless. "Who have you been talking to?" They were as surprised as me. "We haven't spoken to anyone. We just waited by the phone for your call. We didn't want to use the phone."

The following morning, Garry's strength, ability to function, and his quiet yet fun appealing personality returned, just as room service had said the previous night. I believe to this day, without a doubt, that this man was an angel sent by God himself.

As I reflected, my mind searched for answers —

It was a miracle the way we were transported to SOS Medika, not dissimilar to Philip being transported to where the Ethiopian Eunuch was reading God's word (Acts 8:26-40). A moment later would have been too late, as the doctor had voiced.

An angel sent to speak a prophetic word given with authority, dressed as room service at the Hilton Hotel Jakarta.

I pondered: Father God, do You want me to experience Your miraculous ways so that we will be prepared for what is to come? Teach me Lord Your ways and help me to trust in You no matter what the circumstances.

Thank You so much for hearing my cry in the car, "Jesus, I NEED YOU." I believe You are taking me deeper into Yourself. Help me to learn quickly as You trust me with Your miraculous ways.

God, you give me the giggles

...go to the lake and throw out your line.
Take the first fish you catch; open its mouth and
you will find a four-drachma coin...
Matthew 17:27

I read in Matthew 17:24-27 when Peter was asked about paying taxes, Jesus told him to go to the lake, throw a line in and the first fish he caught would have a four-drachma coin in its mouth to pay what was said to be required.

Being a creative person, I love this passage and I laughed out loud at the incredible creativity and out-of-the-box thinking of Jesus. If He used these comical and quirky ways back then, and we read, "Jesus Christ is the same yesterday and today and forever," (Hebrews 13:8) then surely, He can use it again. I believe I experienced His quirkiness, as you will read in this chapter.

From the day our beautiful daughter Kylie was born. she has given us immense pleasure and joy. Garry and I were excited as I went into labour on Sunday night, February 6th. When the first pains started, I heard this new dad-to-be say, "Sit here Princess and I'll make you a cup of tea." How awesome that he remembered what was shared at our pre-natal classes. Very early the following morning, we excitedly drove very fast through streets of Sydney, making our way to King George V Hospital, eagerly anticipating the new era before us.

To this day, I can still see the looks the doctors and all medical staff gave as this slippery bundle made its way into our world. "It's a boy," Garry excitedly announced. Almost laughing out loud, the doctor said, "I think you need to take another look, what you see is the umbilical cord." These words gave us and others many chuckles in the years that followed, so when our next two children were born, Garry looked twice before making the same embarrassing mistake. Our beautiful daughter was born on 7th February 1972. Together we held her, a treasured gift from God. We dedicated Kylie back to Him, believing that in the years to come she would bear much fruit for His kingdom.

As we manoeuvred our way through parenthood, Garry and I prayed much for our three children. Our gorgeous daughter, in her young adult life, helped us grow in the knowledge of what it meant to cling to God. We also held resolutely to His promises with the assurance that He is able as we faced difficult seasons. With the knowledge that is in the following verses, God's word rang true continually, and we never let go.

So do not fear, for I am with you; do not be dismayed, for I am your God.
I will strengthen you and help you; I will uphold you
with my righteous right hand.
Isaiah 41:10

The Lord is my strength and my song; he has given me victory---
Exodus 15:2 NLT

Kylie was a gorgeous little princess, always smiling, always caring, even when she came running out of school one day shouting excitedly, unaware of the people around her, "Mum, I don't have to come to school tomorrow, I have nits!"

Kylie's heart for God at a young age was paramount but she was persecuted for desiring to live a life wholeheartedly for Jesus. When she told me how the boys in her class had tormented her, I was nauseated beyond belief. Each day my heart would ache as I took her to the school gates, knowing what was ahead but I would wrap her in the arms of Jesus.

I shared with Kylie her options: be equally cruel back to them (thinking back, I cannot believe I even suggested this, but it was an option), or you can pray what Jesus prayed from the Cross, "Jesus, forgive them as they don't know what they are doing", knowing that your mum is standing with you and praying for you constantly.

My heart leapt for joy and cried in pain as Kylie, at 11, came out of the school with a face that was radiant, saying, "Mum, I was able to pray for those boys three times today." Yes, my gorgeous Kylie was an overcomer, but at the same time, I knew my precious daughter had had verbal atrocities thrown at her as she prayed for these boys.

Kylie, I believe, was a threat to the kingdom of evil as she was a remarkable missionary at a young age. It was not surprising therefore that on any given afternoon I would see her walking home with someone, and hear her words: "Mum, my friend wants to give her heart to Jesus. Will you pray the prayer with her?"

Our children attended many schools due to our constant moves with Garry's work. At these schools, if there were no weekly Christian meetings, Kylie would go to her school principal and ask permission to organise one. Nothing would stand in her way. If the reply was, "I'm sorry, Kylie, there is no Christian teacher available to oversee a group at this time," Kylie would say, "That's okay, my mum will sit in on the group." Hence, at Alstonville High School and Jakarta International School, a Christian movement began on each campus.

It became obvious that Kylie had Satan working overtime and he nearly won her heart. Anyone reading this knows that with prayer and faith, Satan has no lasting power. He was defeated at Calvary, and we now have victory.

Whilst living in Jakarta, I grew strong in the knowledge of the power God has over darkness due to the many occasions it tried to unleash its ugly work. The power of God through the Holy Spirit is much greater than that of Satan. I was aware of the signs and was always ready for the fight.

We Must Know How to Fight

Kylie graduated and stayed with us one more year before returning to Australia for a position that was offered to her. Not having any friends, Kylie found life difficult. She attended a church close to where she was living and tried hard to be the young lady that God intended her to be. What we found out later was that the young adults at church did not truly have a heart for Jesus. One afternoon, Kylie called us, sobbing from loneliness and lack of friendships. We listened as she poured out her heart. We listened, encouraged and prayed with her. After an hour of talking, we thought the conversation was over and we hung up. A while later, Kylie called back, still crying. It was heartbreaking for me, and I cried with her and to God. No matter how strong I thought I was, and how much I had seen God work in my life, this trial again brought me to my knees. I wanted to rush home and wish I had. However, I would never trade the outcome as I saw God's mighty power ultimately overcome evil once again.

It was at this time that Kylie was invited to attend the local club as a weekly outing. In her loneliness, she accepted this invitation, which was a way to enjoy friendships, especially knowing the ones who had invited her were from the church. As we were living so far away, we did not realise how much Kylie had become involved in this lifestyle until our term in Jakarta ended and we returned home. We came to realise what loneliness and lack of friends and support had done to our beautiful daughter whose heart and spirit had been sold out for Jesus. It saddened me so much that Kylie no longer wanted me to pray aloud, asking for the arms of Jesus and the covering of the Holy Spirit to be around her. I saw the sly smirk of the evil one as if to say, she is now mine. "Lord, I cried out, what has happened to all our prayers? Where is our Kylie who loved and lived for you with a passion?" Garry and I chose to love Kylie unconditionally, not condemning, but loving and encouraging her even though her choices were certainly not wise. I chose to put a rose in her room each week with a note, "We love you, Kylie," and then the fight against the prince of darkness began. Each day, as our treasured Kylie left for work, I would run upstairs two steps at a time and allow praise music to permeate her room throughout the day. I wanted the spirit of praise to fill her room, and for her to literally feel God's presence as she walked in each night. I would take my Bible and walk back and forth in her small room, believing that God's word would be at work. I knew there was a strong wall holding Kylie's heart captive, so each time I prayed or read, I visualised a brick falling off, then a piece of mortar, then another brick, Oh the faith that welled up as I prayed and praised. I became bold and would say, "Satan, you will never have my daughter. She was dedicated to being a mighty woman of God. If you want to sit on the bed and listen then feel free, but you will be listening to the mighty name of Jesus being lifted high and your power will diminish. Every time I pray and praise, your power is lessened, and Kylie is one step closer to Jesus." I never bothered to look as to whether he stayed or went, because I knew the victory was being won in the heavenlies and on earth.

I will give you the keys of the kingdom of heaven; whatever you bind on earth will be bound in heaven, and whatever you loose on earth will be loosed in heaven.
Matthew 16:19

The time I spent walking and praying in Kylie's room was significant. Reading God's word unleashed faith. I knew that allowing the praise music to permeate every nook meant that Kylie would experience the irresistible presence of the Holy Spirit drawing her back into God's kingdom. Peace flows when we intentionally bring God and all he has given to us into our realm.

Our answer was on its way, but at this stage we had not been given eyes to see what lay ahead

One Thursday night, while Garry was overseas, an audacious faith welled up within me; it was so strong that I knew l needed to act immediately. I said to our sons, "Darren and Pete, I'm going over to the Oatley RSL Club where Kylie will be to pray over it, and you can come if you like."

"Sure, mum, we'll come." They knew about the fight I had been waging against the enemy for Kylie.

Armed with my daring faith and a power that is ours, all three of us jumped in the car and drove to the battle ground. Standing across the road from the club, we stretched our hands towards the club, and we prayed for Kylie who at that time was inside. We believed the Holy Spirit would do His work in Kylie as it was Him prompting the action that was set in motion.

As we came home, we stopped at the shops and bought bright green cardboard and put signs all around her room with words like these and many others:

- Kylie, you are our most beautiful daughter
- Kylie, you are the best sister we could ever have
- Kylie, you are so special to our family
- Kylie, as a sister, we love you so much

Many more signs were written placed on the walls. Kylie's room was ablaze with love as we attached a red carnation to every sign.

That night, at around 8.30pm, the front door opened and in walked our beautiful daughter. I was so surprised as her nights at the club always ended much later. "You're home early Kylie !!"

"Mum, I don't know what happened but there came a time when I couldn't stop vomiting so I had to come home."

I could hardly stop myself from laughing and thinking, God that was amazingly creative (hence the title of this chapter), but the miracle did not end there. Since that night, each time Kylie walked into the club, she had the same reaction.

Oh, the POWER when mixed with PRAYER, FAITH and OBEDIENCE!

Our Miracle was Unfolding

As youth leaders, we were taking the young people to a huge outdoor Music Festival called 'Blackstump' for the weekend. Kylie had sold her ticket not wanting to go as the club scene was more enticing. As we drove away, we shared with our beautiful daughter we did not want any male friends staying in our home over the weekend, nor could there be any alcohol or DVD's, of which we did not approve. She agreed. Then Garry, Peter and I drove to the festival, praying for her as each kilometre passed.

That night, Kylie again made her way to the club, and again she was attacked with vomiting. Whilst in the bathroom, all her so-called friends said to each other, "Let's leave before she returns as she is no longer the Kylie we know." One young man said, "We cannot do that to her," just as Kylie returned. Sensing something was amiss due to the uncomfortable silence, Kylie asked, "Is everything okay?"

"We are saying good-bye. All you do of late is spend time in the bathroom. You are no longer the Kylie that's full of fun, doing the things we like to do, so we're leaving." Without another word, all but one left the club. These friends had been her life, and now she had nothing. Feelings of rejection, hopelessness and discouragement swept over her.

One young man stayed (I'll call him Billy) said to Kylie, "What are you going to do now?" Without needing to think, her reply was, "I'm going to a place where I know I'm loved, and if you want to come, I'll pay for you also." Billy had never been to a Christian meeting ever in his life, but he said, "Yes, I'll come with you."

Oh, the joy of answered prayers. Oh. the joy of watching a miracle unfold. Oh, the joy of remembering walking into her bedroom and visualizing the walls which surrounded her crashing down one brick at a time. Oh, the joy of loving unconditionally even when it was not at all easy.

I was reading a book the next morning and what a surprise! "Kylie, so good to see you." There was no time to share details as we were about to go to the morning worship, but we cried and hugged each other. At that moment, disappointment was swept away, love and acceptance replaced hopelessness, and Kylie was embraced in love.

At the worship, some of the young people walked and claimed Kylie for Jesus all over again. Yes, our beautiful Kylie responded to the call of the Holy Spirit that morning, giving her life unreservedly back to Jesus and what's more, Billy gave his life to Jesus also, a double blessing.

After some time, Kylie gave Garry and I a card with this message:

"Thank you for loving me unconditionally, even when you did not agree with what I was doing."

This card with its powerful and loving words meant the world to us. Love speaks volumes when it is unconditional. Was it an easy time? Not in any way, but we held on because we knew the power and truth that was in God's word. I chose never to give up, no matter what obstacles I encountered. Yes, there were tears, yes, there was pain, but there was ultimate joy in the breakthrough.

Kylie never took the signs down that we hung around her room the night that we prayed over the club, nor the carnations. I just picked them up after they died and fell to the floor. The love Kylie felt from her family was overwhelming.

God, you make me laugh, be it a four-drachma coin in the fish's mouth or a daughter vomiting at a club as her family stood across the road praying audaciously. Both answers so very creative, but it is all about HIM.

What an absolute honour it is as we read in Ephesians 2:6, that God raised us up with Christ and seated us with Him in the heavenly realms. He is above all principalities and power and all things are under His feet.

Our God will use the unexpected

Nothing is impossible for God!
Luke 1:37 (CEV)

"No, please stop praying like that!" I laugh so much as I look back at my outburst of words whilst over one hundred awesome young people were praying for Garry and myself at our farewell. We had led the Saturday Night Youth Group in Jakarta and were now returning to Australia.

Three years previously, we had been asked to consider leading this youth group to give Christian young people somewhere to go each Saturday night. Charlie and Kaye White were being transferred back to Singapore which left no-one to continue leading this ministry for expatriate young people.

"I don't believe this is for us as I feel no calling for youth ministry," I said to Garry when the offer was given. We were already leading a Life Group and Garry was on the worship team. Youth leadership was never what I believed to be a passion God had given me, but at the same time we both desired to be where God was leading, whatever that meant.

We both chose to kneel beside our bed and pray, "Lord, if this is what You have for us, and it's Your plan, please equip us with every gift that we will need."

As we stood up, the Holy Spirit impressed on us, look around at the house I have blessed you with, big enough for Darren and Peter to ride their skateboards inside, perfect for a youth group.

This prayer brought about the beginning of a work in youth leadership which spanned the following 14 years. It was so unexpected, and we certainly felt unqualified. I praise God that it was incredibly and powerfully blessed and anointed as it grew numerically and spiritually beyond our wildest dreams.

Looking back at this God ordained work in Jakarta, where we saw many young people come to know and love Jesus wholeheartedly, and many who are now in ministry all over the world. Julian, one of the young men only this week recently wrote and then called to say he was being ordained as a Pastor and that it all started back in our home in Jakarta.

An hour before each meeting, some of these young people would join Garry and I in prayer, therefore we were not surprised to experience incredible miracle healings, and young people coming to know Jesus each week, and see them weep after the meeting in repentance. The joy it was to see many young people leading their friends to a faith in Jesus that would last for eternity.

Prayer groups were starting everywhere on the school campus, before school, during lunch times and free periods. These kids were on fire, and the words used were "Revival has broken out".

A Christmas production that we organised was held in the school theatre. Being international, the school, initially did not give us consent to go ahead with using their venue due to the presence of many different religious groups attending. They did not want to appear to favour the Christian faith. Not taking no for an answer, more young people came early to pray that this event would be allowed to proceed as they wanted their friends to experience the love of Jesus they had come to know. Everyone prayed and believed, and our answer came, permission was finally given. Missionaries from all over Java who had heard about the production attended, bringing along their rebellious non-Christian teenagers, some of whom cried in repentance that night.

God blessed this Saturday Night Youth Group more than we could have ever believed possible

Now, after four years in Jakarta, God was leading us back to Australia. On our last night of youth, some 120 amazing full-of-the-Spirit expatriate young people laid their hands on us, and prayed, "Lord, as Garry and Lynn return to Australia, open a way for them to continue this work of leading young people to know You, and the miracles we have powerfully seen."

As I shared in the opening sentence, my words were: "No!!! we have loved each of you so much, but I don't believe we will lead another Youth Group in Australia. Maybe a Life Group, or a ladies' and men's ministry but not Youth."

How Jesus must have laughed along with His Father God as they peered into our future, whilst listening to my objections. Little do they know what is in store for them, thought Jesus, as I foolishly uttered these words without consulting the Master Planner. There is yet more work, more challenges, more blessings, more kids to love, as you give your future to Me, and you have already been equipped. I'm sure Daddy God and Jesus could not wait to share their plans with us. It was just as well we were unable to hear and see Heaven's joy and read God's thoughts that had been laid out for all the saints to see but still awaited us.

After settling into our newly purchased home in the Sutherland Shire of Sydney and returning to our church at Lugarno, it was time to again pray about our future ministry.

As was our practice, Garry and I took each other's hands, signifying we were one, knelt on our lounge room floor and prayed, "Precious Jesus, thank You for all Your miraculous leading over the past years, we are here again to ask what You have for us to do as we start this new era at Lugarno."

Oh, what joy I believe was on the face of Jesus as he ran through Heaven excitedly saying, "Dad, can you hear what they are asking — what would we have them do? We knew that would be their prayer." As our prayer went up, I believe Heaven's joy was unleashed.

It was during that week, due to the youth group going through difficult times, that most of the leaders in the younger age group (Years 7 to 10) had chosen to resign, with only two remaining. The older youth and young adults were also struggling, and it saddened me to learn that the older young people were involved in any sin you cared to name.

With excitement in our spirits, we approached the pastor with our heartfelt prayer, unaware of all that had transpired. Looking back, it still makes me laugh that we were about to be asked to do what I had stopped these Spirit-filled young people from praying back in Jakarta four months earlier.

As we sat down with our pastor, he shared with us what was in his heart, and the quandary he faced in the youth ministry. "Garry and Lynn, with your experience in youth ministry in Jakarta, would you be willing to take on the younger youth and also work with Rod in the older young people, as well as overseeing the whole of our youth ministry?"

The prayers of those treasured kids back in Jakarta rang in my ears. When the Abrahams return to Australia, allow them to continue this same ministry of what has happened here, where many have come to know Jesus and are now powerfully living for him.

Our ministry in Lugarno was launched. What awaited us was unexpected. It was as if the evil one discouraged us at every turn and was gleefully glaring and laughing at the free reign he had been allowed to pursue.

Thank you, Jesus, for Your awesome enabling and anointing which allowed us to endure. What is written in Ephesians 3:20 (my translation), "…more than we could ever ask, think, dream or imagine…" was about to unfold.

"Is there vodka in that punch on the table?" I was asked on the first night of youth by a 13-year-old young lady, to which I answered "No."

"Well, it must be disgusting," came her reply. Peter our son came home crying, "I don't want to go back to that youth group again." James, a 12-year-old young man who had broken his arm came to us saying he would not be back until his arm was healed, worried about what the boys would do to him. No one would bring their friends because of the actions of this group. The language and profanity that flowed would match that heard in any local night club, tyres on our car let down during the meeting and this was the younger youth.

After the first night Garry put away his guitar as we became very aware that what was shared in Indonesia was to be put aside for a time at Lugarno. We began to understand why previous young leaders had resigned. Darren, our son who was in the older group, was relentlessly humiliated for bringing his Bible to youth and church. None of these insights had been shared with us when we were asked to take the position.

Those first few months were certainly not easy and there were times when I wanted to say, Lord, it's all too hard. On two occasions, I went to the car ready to go, or run to the pastor to say, "No more," and both times, for whatever reason, I happened to check my mailbox on my way out. Both times there was a card from Yanti, one of the young people in Jakarta, which said, "Garry and Lynn, just to let you know I'm praying for you both in your work with the youth at Lugarno." Both times, I went back inside and fell on my knees. "What is your plan, Lord?" Garry and I cried out. So clearly the answer was given.

"Love these young people, love them unconditionally, show them my love like they have never known before. Put your arms around them and let them know how valued they are."

During one precious and sensitive moment, a 13-year-old young man shared with me as tears welled up in his eyes whilst playing a colour game. "Lynn, my favourite colour is black, because my whole world is black." We were seeing another dimension to the youth that God had placed in our care.

"Where do we start?" was the cry of our hearts. We want these youth to love You, know You, live for You and praise You.

The Stage Was Set to Release a Miracle

We asked Rod, who was leading the 18 years and above if he would join us each week as we believed that it was only through prayer that we would see a breakthrough in the lives of these young people. Each Tuesday morning, from 5.00am to 7.00am, Rod, Garry and I would be on our knees, lifting these youth up to God, praying that He could pave the way in what seemed at the time a very challenging situation. We prayed and we loved these kids unconditionally, and we never gave up, knowing God was faithful.

There were two verses that we held on to steadfastly every Tuesday morning—

Nothing is impossible with God!
Luke 1:37 (CEV)

Let us not become weary in doing good, for at the proper time we will reap a harvest if we do not give up.
Galatians 6:9

I typed theses verses out and we held them as we prayed:

- Knowing our God is faithful
- Knowing He is true to His word

- Knowing these young people are worth every prayer
- Knowing we would see the victory

Our lounge room became a place where God met us as we interceded so these young people would become `trophies for Jesus.'

One Sunday night, three new non-Christian young people walked into the church. They were dressed immaculately, with hearts open and hungry for truth. We were accustomed to seeing our young people with long black hair and dressed in black, with no life in their eyes and no hunger for God.

Adam, Lara and Steve were like a fresh aroma and endeared themselves immediately to the group. These three young people desired to know the God who was faithfully preached. All three came to know and love Jesus and gave their whole life unreservedly to Him and were baptised. One of the young men asked, "After your baptism, do you want to go the pub to celebrate?" to which they answered, "No, that doesn't interest us." These sincere young people stood resolutely for God and the decision they had made, and vigilantly delved into His Word.

Darren who had been humiliated for bringing his Bible to church was encouraged as his persistent prayer for more on-fire young people to show up was now being answered. Our awesome and wonderful God was responding and giving us eyes to see each move He made.

Creative, imaginative and ingenious are the words to describe how God chose three non-Christian young people and Darren to become the catalyst in the process of loosening Satan's grip on these young people for such a long time.

Tuesday mornings became a time when we not only prayed but celebrated by lifting our hands and voices in praise. Unrivalled joy filled our lounge room in those sacred early morning hours where audacious faith soared and miracles rose in our minds and spirits for these young people.

God was also sifting the younger group in their love for Jesus. We saw an increase in numbers as these precious young ones were now inviting their friends and introducing them to Jesus. Black evil situations were turning into light as the Spirit began to permeate the lives of these cherished youth. Repentance and tears became normal as hearts were softened and changed.

7.00am Saturday morning prayer meetings began in the local park for those who desired to pray for their friends. On those frosty winter mornings their prayers would ring out touching heaven. We shivered but our hearts were hot with the Spirit.

Sunday night suppers after church were a highlight and became powerful encouraging testimony times. Often sick people from the church were invited to come. The young people prayed over them, and healing followed. One gentleman who was given a short time to live was invited. It was as if the roof lifted and heaven poured in. This man died many years later of old age. Faith rose in the lives of these transformed kids.

Prior to our youth camps, whole or half nights of prayer became normal. To see this group of young people now desiring to take a half-hour time slot, leading their peers who came to pray, excited about the joy of their changed lives. What a gift to be in the presence of these young people when, even at 3.00am, praise filled the room and rang out into the darkness.

It was no surprise to see the lives of so many changed for eternity. We were seeing young people now going on mission trips, and year after year young people would sleep on our floor or wherever they could find a spot as we attended a week-long Christian conference in Sydney, Australia.

I laughed to myself as I quietly shared with God during the Youth Leadership Stream I attended. "Look, I am the oldest person in this stream by a long way." I was not impressed as I saw Jesus walk away putting His hands over His ears. He then turned and said, "Lynn, I'm not looking at your age, I'm looking for your obedience as you use the gifts I have placed within you. I will take you out when the time is right. Just be who I have called you to be, and you will continue to see miracles like you never thought possible."

How precious was the night when we invited the young people to come together, laying their parents' names on the altar, praying for their salvation. What joy it was for those young people to see the outcome as parents came to know Jesus. Oh, can I say, the joy we experienced as we saw their faith growing.

Various weekends were arranged, where we were privileged to witness these young people being set free from deep inner hurts, sickness, addictions and demonic influence, where we talked about Godly relationships and preparation for marriage. These young people were now desiring to be wholeheartedly sold out for Jesus in every area of their lives.

I believe that a God-given initiative turned out to be pivotal in the history of the church and the youth. I photographed every young person and put their photos on boards with their names. I then shared with the church if they would like to take one photo and covenant to pray daily for that young person. There was a scurry after church as the older adults hovered around the boards and selected a photo or two. What a blessing this was for the youth. Those who took the photos let the young people know that they were praying for them. These kids now had spiritual parents and grandparents who loved, prayed, cared, and took an interest in them. This exercise bridged the gap between the old and young which was immensely valued by both generations.

With all the amazing changes in these beautiful young people who had risen from the ashes, now shone radiating the love of Jesus. We confidently asked if they could be given the opportunity to take a night service, and the answer was an overwhelming yes!

The church was not only packed to capacity but overflowed – parents and friends sandwiched on the pews, standing in doorways or anywhere they could find a spot, even standing on chairs at the back so they could see, and those not able to gain entry peered through the windows.

The youth led the service. Powerful testimonies were shared on what God had done in their lives. They preached and sang, girls danced with a purity and reverence not seen before.

During this service tears flowed uncontrollably as the presence of God fell powerfully touching those who came. Lives were given to Jesus, bondages broken as the Holy Spirit past by every chair, doorway and window. Other nights such as these followed.

With all the beautiful godly miraculous changes we saw in the lives of these precious young people, we never stopped stepping into the throne room of Heaven on those Tuesday mornings – the power that flowed as three leaders believed tenaciously that God could perform what He had promised as we still held onto His Word.

• • • • • • •

From a group that was anything but godly, to one where Jesus radiated in all His fullness.

Lara, one of the non-Christians who came to church, later became a youth leader and is now a pastor in this church.

Darren, who was humiliated for bringing his Bible, also became a youth leader and is now a pastor in a large Pentecostal church on Vancouver Island, Canada.

Darrin, who was one of the youth leaders who supported us faithfully for many years in leadership, has not long stood down from youth ministry.

Lisa, one of those young people who we never stopped loving, is now living in Milan, Italy, with her family supporting a Christian Pentecostal ministry in this country.

There are too many more to mention, but many have gone on to serve God in mission work, youth, children's ministry, medical positions, worship teams, on pastoral teams and holding high positions of influence in the corporate world. In absolute humility as tears stream down my face, I give all praise to a faithful God who honoured our prayers and lifted these kids from the dirt and filth of the gutter to the absolute unbridled joy of knowing Jesus and using their talents for Him.

Jakarta Youth Group — many of these young people also went on to become pastors, missionaries, youth leaders and worship leaders, and others too many to mention. Their hearts cried out – we love you God and want to give our lives as a sacrifice of praise.

I love you God more than I can ever put into words.
You are magnificient, eternally wonderful, you are my God.

My dad saw pink flowers

Faith was unleashed as my dad had been blind for three years

I will praise you, Lord, with all my
heart and tell about the wonders you have worked.
Psalms 9:1 (CEV)

Dad can see, Dad can see!" came my mother's excited voice over the phone. The reason for my mum's excitement was my dad had been blind for the past three years.

I loved my dad very much. It was he who demonstrated to me a trust in God that I will never forget. He absolutely delighted in God's creation and taught me the same. He cherished the beautiful God-formed shells found on the sand or those he bought in specialised shops. He would place a shell or a flower on the palm of his hand and say, "Lynn, look at the beauty of God's creation."

My dad was the eldest of three boys, and sadly, his father was hospitalised permanently, hence my godly grandmother had no option but to take my dad out of school at 12 years to seek employment so he could help provide for the family.

During the Great Depression, money and employment were scarce and not much work available for a 12-year-old, but my grandmother's trust in God was paramount, no matter the economic climate. My father's uncle who was a shoe repairer offered my dad the opportunity to learn this trade, which was an amazing answer to Grandma's prayer, even though it was some distance from where they lived.

I still find it difficult to comprehend the idea of a young boy having to travel five hours daily to his newly acquired job. Each day my dad walked, travelled by bus, train and ferry on those dark, cold, lonely morning and nights. Necessity compelled my dad to hold onto God, as his mum had faithfully taught him. He also learned what it was to be content as he was unable to accomplish his own dreams and aspirations. After some time, my dad was able to live with his uncle which was a wonderful provision.

After marrying my mum, dad acquired his own business much closer to home. However, lack of good wiring and insurance due to shortage of money led to disastrous outcomes when he encountered three fires in his shop. Yet, during these trying times of needing to start over again and again, his quiet spirit, and his trust and faith in God were undeniable. I listened and watched my dad and mum each night read God's word together and surrender everything to Him. I was learning to trust without question.

At school, dad was told he had the intellect to become a physician or a similar profession, but due to his circumstances, was unable to follow this path. Choosing not to allow these obstacles to bring discouragement, he turned to God who opened a way for him to live his dream. Dad attained a university degree in business management in his early fifties, graduating with a high distinction average, which enabled him to enter the public service.

My sister and I grew up not knowing the riches of this world, but what we did know was the riches that money could never buy. Our Christmas and birthday presents were usually toys obtained from the garbage tip or wherever mum and dad could find gifts that could be repaired or recycled. As a child and even during my teenage years, I never appreciated what my parents did to give us their best.

I remember shrieking with joy one Christmas morning to find under the tree a sparkling red three-wheeler bike which my dad had spent hours restoring. Another year, my dad-built my sister Colleen and myself an amazing shop which gave us so many happy playing hours. Dad and mum never shared with us that money was scarce but I never felt I missed out. Due to their wisdom we grew up in an atmosphere of abundant security, love and joy. As I look back, these attributes were worth more to me than any physical possession. I watched daily their trust in God and seeing their everyday needs being continually met.

I pray that God will take care of all your needs with the wonderful blessings that come from Christ Jesus!
Philippians 4:19 (CEV)

Looking back, as a child and teenager, I knew my dad and mum would have stood firmly and camped on this verse many times.

As I grew older, I became very aware of the blessing they were to many people and the joy they brought, especially to the widows who had no-one to help them.

I still remember much of what dad taught me, and as an adolescent I would occasionally mock him, but the wisdom of his teaching has stayed with me. My dad knew his Bible well and loved the teachings of the "Great Apostle Paul" (as he would call him). Some of his favourite sayings were:

- *"Lynn do not be a slave to what this world offers,"* as he referred to my love for fashion and being fashionable.
- *"Lynn, the Great Apostle Paul teaches 'to be content with what you have, not continually wanting more'."* I appreciated this as he was a role model himself in this regard daily.
- *"Lynn, the Great Apostle Paul teaches us 'to flee from evil, run as fast as you can'."* When I was asked at work to go to a séance, these words came racing back to me. Remembering my dad's words certainly protected me as I listened to the fear in those who attended when they shared their experiences the following morning. My dad's words also helped in many other circumstances in my life where I was exposed to various temptations.

In his later years, my dad became blind due to glaucoma and macular degeneration. My mum looked after him until he had a major fall. After his operation, he was placed in a nursing home.

Throughout his adversity, he never once complained or stopped ministering. He knew the footsteps of all the cleaners, doctors and nurses. He would ask them with a smile how their day was and listened. Often with tears flowing, they would share the difficulties they were experiencing. My elderly blind dad would take their hand and sensitively pray for each one. They loved his care, and they would always share with me how valued he made them feel. My dad did not need a building to minister, his room was his church. Power would flow as he prayed in that nursing home, and I know it melted the heart of Jesus.

During one of my regular visits dad heard my footsteps, his voice echoed loudly through those corridors, "Lynn did you bring Wigglesworth?"

Smith Wigglesworth was a very old gentleman who authored many books on faith, healing and the Holy Spirit. I would read one of those long chapters from these books each time I visited him, and together we were learning much.

One visit in April 2002, I had just finished reading a chapter when I felt an incredible surge of faith rise within me as I thought of the blind man that Jesus healed in John 9. In this account the disciples asked him, "*.... Rabbi, who sinned, this man or his parents, that he was born blind?" "Neither this man nor his parents sinned," said Jesus, "but this happened so that the works of God might be displayed in him..." After saying this, he spat on the ground, made some mud with the saliva, and put it on the man's eyes. "Go," he told him, "Wash in the Pool of Siloam." So the man went and washed, and he came home seeing.*

With faith supernaturally rising, I bent over close to dad and said, "Dad, would you allow me put my spit on your eyes as Jesus did to the blind man recorded in John, and pray for you?" Instantly my dad replied, "Yes Lynn, please." Without thinking of the ramifications of what I was doing, but just unleashing a faith that had risen within me, I spat on my hand and wiped the saliva on dad's eyes and said, "Dad, be healed in Jesus' name."

What a precious dad who would allow his daughter to place spit on his eyes, it still makes me smile and even laugh. I was running late for an appointment so after this faith filled act and prayer, I kissed my dad and left, leaving the outcome to our wonderful God.

Two hours later, my mum arrived at the nursing home as she did each afternoon. She took her seat next to dad and held his hand while he quietly spoke. "Nell is there a large window over there in the wall?" pointing to a window close by. "Yes Fred," my mum answered.

"Outside the window, is there a tree with many beautiful pink flowers?" my dad asked.

"Can you see them; can you see them?" my mum excitedly asked.

"Yes, Nell, I can see them, I can see God's beautiful creation. God has given me my sight in answer to Lynn's prayer, I can see," dad said in awe and wonder.

I cannot remember what else was said that afternoon, but mum rang us all when she arrived home after her visit, filled with elation. "Dad has been healed of his blindness! He can see again! I sat with him, and he could see." The following day, we all made our way to the home full of eagerness, but dad's sight had not remained. That night, at a family dinner, my mum enthusiastically told us about the visit where dad was again able to see. We laughed at the way it all happened, putting spit on Dad's eyes. How audacious. We praised God with all that was within us.

During the exhilaration, the phone rang. It was a nurse from my dad's nursing home. "I'm so sorry, Mr. Gray has just passed away. He was feeling unwell, so I put him into bed. I told him that I would be back after I had finished my rounds. I returned 20 minutes later, and he was gone. Again, I am so sorry."

I did not find his death easy, but at the same time I felt joy for what my dad experienced in his last moments on earth. He was able to see the beauty of those pink flowers, God's creation, and my mum whom he adored.

Even though my dad's sight was short-lived, the faith that rose within me that day was something I will never forget.

From the time I came to know of Jesus, I have never doubted His power. As I have quoted many times in this book, our God is able to do abundantly more than I can ever think, dream or imagine, and I knew then what I know now, I can trust Him.

I will trust him, I will not doubt, I will use the gifts that he has given to me for his glory.

The impossible becomes a reality

I am the Lord, the God of all mankind.
Is anything too hard for me?
Jeremiah 32:27

What is impossible with men
is possible with God.
Luke 18:27

The verses introducing this chapter came running to my mind as if they had the legs of an athlete, "Lynn, another opportunity for you to see my miraculous ways in action," I believed God excitedly spoke to me.

It started like this. I was driving to my favourite shopping mall, for a quiet coffee, then to buy some essentials. At the time, I was listening to a CD, 'Samson's hair is growing again', which was an intriguing passage as we read in the book of Judges chapters 13 through 16.

My mobile phone rang. I pulled over to the side of the road and immediately recognised my son Darren's voice.

"Mum, will you pray for Kristy and me?" That sure caught my attention as God loves it when His children call out for help, trusting Him with their struggles, disappointments, sharing joys and allowing Him to be a part of everyday life. "Tell me more Darren," I asked.

Sensitively he began. "Mum, Kristy and I would love to have a family, but there are some medical difficulties, and it doesn't look good for us; in fact it may even be impossible. I know God is able, but I sure would like to have some support as we walk this path. Please mum, will you stand with us both?"

Listening to these heartfelt words and the ache they carried, my mind flashed back at the excitement Garry and I experienced as Darren, a squirmy bundle, entered our world in a rush.

• • • • • • •

Darren was a quieter child, but he always displayed an unusually sensitive spirit towards God and spiritual things. One Sunday, at a church service, Darren, who was only three, wanted to take communion. His dad quietly whispered, "No". Garry then tried to explain to him as the bread and grape juice passed by when a deep cry of anguish rose within him, not a cry of anger but one of deep distress. At the conclusion of the service, one of the older spiritual men of the church came and asked what had happened. We shared the situation and this man revealed, "I believe Darren, as young as he is, has an understanding unique to a child his age. I believe you need to let him take part in this service as I truly believe he has been given insight, even at three."

At six, Darren would accompany Garry to the 6.00am prayer meeting each Sunday morning at Dubbo Baptist Church. Then, at seven, Darren asked if he could be baptised, saying he wanted to follow Jesus, whatever or wherever that path may lead. Ultimately, at ten, he followed Jesus in baptism.

The song that he chose to be sung as he rose from the water—

"I will praise you in all my ways
I will live for you through all of my days
That your majesty, glory and power
Will be seen upon the earth
I will praise you in all my ways
I will live for you through all of my days
That your majesty, glory and power
Will be seen upon the earth."[4]

As Darren grew, he began displaying a beautiful way of quietly encouraging others, and to this day people marvel at the source of his kindness. As a sensitive and gifted worship and youth leader, he has impacted many people, both young and old. He completed his degree in radiation therapy, an area that enabled him to again show his compassion. Later, he acquired a Master's in Counselling after experiencing much grief when his beloved dad and hero went to be with Jesus. God in all His glory was continually demonstrated in his life.

Darren loved God passionately and God was paramount in his life. He also knew that prayer was the answer to all he encountered, so for him to be reaching out now meant that this setback was something that needed another level of help.

"Absolutely Darren, I'll be praying," as I focussed back on what he had asked. Immediately faith surged within my spirit and an eagerness to see their desire come to be.

Yes, we can pray with anticipation when we bring God into the equation, trusting Him as our audacious faith is unleashed and set in motion. After this interaction, coffee and shopping were no longer on my agenda. I had to pray for a baby to be brought into this world.

How awesome, another opportunity to again see and experience God's power being set free for the world to see. Another little person to spread Your Word and live for You.

My heart was full of compassion as I felt the disappointment that Darren and Kristy were experiencing. As a mum, I had the urge to immediately book a flight to Brisbane, put my arms around them and let them know I cared and that we would stand together. At that moment, sadness at what had just been shared crept into my spirit.

I smile and sometimes giggle when the Holy Spirit steps in ever so quickly, not allowing me time to wallow in this kind of thinking. He is quick to remind me of the time when the Great King David returned from battle to find his campsite had been plundered, with his two wives and families of his men captured and taken away. This Great King, God's anointed, wept aloud at what had taken place and upon hearing that his men were wanting to stone him. Tired and exhausted, with a heavy heart, God's word quotes: "*... but David found strength in the Lord his God." 1 Samuel 30:6.*

How good is our God. He had allowed me to listen to the encouraging CD just prior to Darren's call. I remember taking those next few moments, like King David, and reminded myself how mighty, how great, how all-knowing our God is. He knew this phone call would be made even before the beginning of time. He knew the difficulty that Darren and Kristy would experience, and it certainly did not catch Him by surprise. God knew what was to be, but allowed it, wanting His kids to see that this blip in the road would make them stronger for what they would face in the future, as they saw His power come to be.

I am known for my fast driving but on this day as I started the car, I had purpose. So great was the faith that had arisen that my coffee was put on hold. Arriving at the mall, I parked the car and ran through the car park and up the escalators, not taking notice of anyone who might have been wondering why this crazy lady was rushing as there were no fire sirens and no one chasing her. When under God's instruction, others do not understand. Breathlessly but incredibly excited, I headed straight to the baby section wanting to look for the most beautiful little outfit that, in the days and months ahead, would carry a great anointing. "Yes, this is the one," I thought as I picked up this little item. As if it was worth a million dollars, I carried it to the cashier knowing that this little piece of clothing was special as it had been a God inspired thought.

When I got home, I laid the little outfit on the bed. I knew what I had to do. Going to the cupboard I reached for the oil. From that day onwards, I knelt and anointed the little outfit with oil and called forth a baby into Kristy's womb.

As I wrote previously, we were unable to walk this road closely with them, and it made my heart ache. Knowing that distance is not an obstacle for God, so to walk this path with Him became an honour and privilege as each day I stepped into His throne room in prayer.

As the days and months passed, the little outfit became a real source of expectancy, a faith builder. Daily, as I prayed and anointed it with oil, I visualised my God-given grandchild wearing it, knowing this baby had been prayed into existence. *What an encouragement the Word of God is.* The Holy Spirit continually brought to my mind when He opened the womb of Hannah and little Samuel was given to her. Again, Sarah and Abraham were given Isaac, and what a gift he was. Then the Holy Spirit said, Lynn, there are more! Rachel and Jacob who were Joseph's parents and of course Elizabeth in her older years became the mother of John the Baptist.

What is impossible with men, is possible with God.
Luke 18:27

Imagine my absolute joy, elation, delight and happiness and any other word that captured the moment when we were told Kristy was pregnant, not just pregnant but with twins! I remember so clearly the words that the Holy Spirit gave me that day, "Lynn, it's a Double Blessing." The words were as clear to me as if said to me by a tangible person.

Darren and Kristy were going out to dinner on what would be one of their last dates prior to these little gifts being born. It was Darren's birthday and they had planned a romantic dinner date at the Summit Restaurant, overlooking Brisbane at night.

Just as they were about to leave for their date, relishing the celebration at this beautiful restaurant with its exquisite food and romantic views, Kristy's waters began to break. I am sure you are smiling, and rightly so. Yes, a phone call needed to be made. I am sure the host of the Summit had never heard, and I believe never will hear, the words that Kristy spoke sweetly to him that night. "I'm so sorry, are you able to hold our reservation for a little while as we need to go to the hospital, but we will be there as soon as we can." I still smile at those innocent and naïve words.

The following day, 8th May 2005, Cody and Sierra were born and placed in humidicribs. I know Darren and Kristy gave praise to God for those who had prayed as they saw and experienced the absolute faithfulness of a miracle working God. In the same miraculous way God answered the heart's desire of Hannah, Sarah, Rachel, Elizabeth and many others, He also was to Darren and Kristy. I experienced my faith being set free in unbridled optimism, even when doctors had said there may be no hope. There is always hope when we take our difficulties to God. Put on our spiritual blinkers and look into the eyes of Jesus. I see Him leaning in to listen. I see Him standing up to receive our requests. I see him thanking us for our trust. I see Him handing what we give to Him over to His father as he intercedes for us, then we rest in the peace and knowledge of His promises.

This chapter is my reflection: It was a privilege to pray and have a son who trusted God enough to ask the question: "Mum, will you stand with us, as we so want to have a family and it doesn't look possible." Medical specialists say it may not be possible, with prayer, faith and trust, God says, "All things are possible."

LORD, you are my God; I will exalt you and praise your name,
for in perfect faithfulness you have done wonderful things,
things planned long ago.
Isaiah 25:1

Dr. Breezy and his disbelief

Then you will call upon me and come and pray to me, and I will listen to you.
Jeremiah 29:12

"Who is Garry Abrahams?" came the loud voice of a nurse as she entered the operating theatre. "Is he a king? How important is this man?" she asked, as she viewed 13 bags of blood hanging on the wall. In her career as a theatre nurse, she had never seen a sight like this. "Garry is one of the nicest men you will ever meet," came the reply of another nurse as the operation proceeded.

In February 2008, Garry and I moved to Brisbane as some of our children had already moved to this beautiful sunshine state and were saying, "Dad and mum, where are you? We are here because you said you were moving and you haven't come. We are waiting for you."

Garry daydreamed of having a house on a canal with a boat tied to a jetty so he could take his grandchildren for rides. He imagined himself sitting under the stars reading Bible stories to them, sharing the absolute magnificance of God, and doing things that grandchildren loved to do. Their remarkable Pa just wanted to feed into their lives and spoil them as that was what he believed a Pa and Nanna were born to do. Unleashing joy and fun with our grandchildren is truly a gift.

As we prepared to move, Garry began to experience pains in his back and legs. After consulting our doctor in Sydney, he was diagnosed as having sciatic nerve pain and medication and exercises were prescribed.

Moving from Sydney into my sister's place in Brisbane, his pain grew so intense he was unable to walk. We were up night after night as I massaged his back and legs. I was almost carrying him wherever he needed to go. I even banged on the supermarket doors early one

Sunday morning, crying and begging them to open so we could buy medication. The pain was intense and no relief came. Were we naive? Looking back, yes, absolutely we were, but we knew no doctor due to our recent move and still believed it to be sciatic nerve pain as we had been told.

One night, my sister who had just returned from holidays heard us and said, "That's it, I'm taking you to the hospital." On our arrival, nurses and doctors surrounded Garry, blood samples were taken, morphine was administered and the pain lessened. The concerned doctor spoke, "Garry, we will not release you until we know what's happening."

The next day, a barrage of questions were asked and we did not understand why. Then with a look of concern the doctor gave us the diagnosis – acute myeloid leukaemia, a very rare and aggressive strand of eosinophilic leukaemia. So rare was this strand that this world renowned haematologist had only ever come across it twice, with Garry being his second case, hence there was limited data available at the time and the reason for all the questions. Dr. John Bashford said, "I'm so sorry, I wish the news could have been different." Garry answered, "Don't be sorry, I just want to say thank you for all you're doing. You watch and see what my God will do."

Over the next five months of hospitalization, my treasured husband underwent chemotherapy and endured horendous side-effects. As a result, we could not develop friendships in Brisbane or find a church home. I praise God for Albany Hills Christian Church (now Emerge) where Kylie, Wayne, Alex and Amy were attending. These amazing people, who did not know us, gave their support even though we could not attend the services at this time.

Over the months that followed, Garry was never well enough to travel which had been our dream. His family had taken him to many places in Queensland as a child. He was looking forward to sharing these locations with me as we fantacised going on a million honeymoons. Yet God again was good, and during a couple of months of remission, due to a bone marrow transplant, we were able to find and ultimately buy our own beautiful home. Garry loved working outdoors, and it was as if he was given supernatural strength to do much around our new home.

In the low times, God still brought unexpected gifts in the form of Pastor Ian Parker and Pastor Fred Evans who came to visit. I still laugh when I recall each time I answered the door and these two men would greet me with huge smiles on their faces and arms outstretched, and they would say, "We are here. We've come to carry the burden." They sat with us, loved us, listened, shared communion, prayed, empathised, encouraged, shared their crazy jokes and lightened our situation. What a joy and a gift these two men were.

Garry and I chose not to view this sickness negatively but rather focus on our God being over all and the knowledge that Jesus had already taken everything to the cross long ago. We put on our spiritual blinkers and looked into the eyes of Jesus who had given us everything we needed. We were very aware of what was happening in Garry's body, and were also very aware that some thought we were living in denial as we saw their whispers but we chose to see it as faith, and that was the way we lived. We wanted to each day enjoy all the blessings that God was giving.

We read God's word, sang (as Garry had an amazing voice), shared communion daily, went for a coffee when we were able, spoke out confidently God's promises, blessed others and always held eachother tightly in this trial.

Then a truly difficult time came and again Garry was rushed back to hosptial for a few months. These times were tough, and I would return to my sister's place as it was closer to the Wesley Hospital. I loved getting up each morning and walking around their pool, singing loudly so negativity and fear would not have a place in my soul. Not having friends in Brisbane, I had asked family and friends in Sydney to send photos and I placed them on the wall of Garry's room. We saw them as our own valued congregation. I purchased a small sound system so God's word or praise songs could fill his hospital room every moment, it made such a difference that even the medical staff commented. I will share in another chapter the miracle that happened because of the continual presence of God.

One morning in December 2008, just prior to Christmas, I sat with Garry as the Infectious Disease Specialist entered the room, "We are going to operate this afternoon, but Garry, there is no way you will pull through this operation."

I was flabbergasted, how could this doctor come in with such horrific news, speaking out in such a pessimistic way? I will call him Dr. Breezy as this was the nickname, I gave to him. He would just breeze in, share what needed to be said and breeze out again.

After hearing his statement, I said, "You may be the doctor, but you have no idea the God who is ours, and you just see what He can do in this operation." I must admit he was lost for words and after a moment's pause, he said. "No, I don't know your God, but I do know Garry has no immunity due to the amount of chemotherapy he is receiving and how very sick he is." This doctor then told us of the virus that was affecting the sinuses of patients whose immunity was compromised. He went on to say they would operate, but with Garry's lack of immunity and weakened body, it would be best for us to say our goodbyes. Garry and I were at peace as I sent a text message to all our friends in Sydney and to the intercessors of Albany Hills Christian Church sharing what had been said and asking for the mighty power of our God to intervene.

I called Kylie and Darren, who came immediately to the hospital and Peter was on the first flight out of Sydney. With a faith in God that was soaring, we prayed that Garry would come through this operation and show Dr. Breezy our God.

Garry was then taken to the operating theatre, our peace remained as those 13 bags of blood hung on the wall.

An Unstoppable Miracle is Set in Motion

A few hours later, with the operation complete, we visited Garry in the intensive care unit. I want to share with everyone reading this that our God is great; our God is mighty; our God has again showed us and our doctor friend that He is able. Not one bag of blood was used, even though Garry was neutropenic (no immunity): this was a miracle and every doctor agreed.

Three days later, after another Magnetic Resonance Imaging was taken, the doctors saw that the sinister aggressive virus had returned. It is one of the worst viruses known in the medical profession because it travels at a rapid pace from the sinuses to the brain, eating whatever that stands in its way. Our family was called into a meeting. This time the surgeon, who was also a professor, said there was a decision to be made. We were told of the prognosis and the devastation of what was before us. We were asked if we wanted to let Garry go. If not, they would operate, taking half of my Garry's face. I looked at the sadness as my children processed this horrendous news.

We were faced with an horrific decision. "I love my dad so much, even with half a face I still want my dad." Peter's words echoed those of Kylie, with a heart that was breaking. At the time Darren's profession was a radiation therapist, and he had seen so much pain during his everyday work career that he did not want to put his dad through more than he was already enduring. He slowly said, "I too love my dad. I love dad more than words can say, but I am willing to let him go into the arms of Jesus who he loves so much, but like you Peter and Kylie, my heart aches so badly."

It was an unimaginable time, one that I do not believe anyone should experience, but God was with us, and we knew His presence.

Each of my children then looked at me and almost together said, "Mum what are your feelings?" All I could think to say was, "I want to ask your dad what he would like." So together we went to Garry who already knew what the doctors were proposing. I asked my beautiful man whom I loved so much, "Garry, what are you thinking?" With absolutely no thought for himself he said, "Princess, (his special name for me,) even with half a face, I want to live. My greatest desire is to share Jesus with my grandchildren. I want to read to them the stories of the great men and women in the Bible and let them know that Jesus can be their Lord and Saviour, that no matter what happens in life, God is greater, God is so good."

Hence the decision was made. With no time to waste due to the severity of this hideous virus, Garry was wheeled along the corridors to the operating room where we gave hugs and kisses and prayed to our ever-faithful God. Then the doors closed behind him.

We gathered as family outside those doors knowing prayer was our only answer. My sister's family joined us, and together we started to pray aloud. We read God's word, we sang and we trusted knowing that:

**Our God is able, our God is true to His word,
and nothing is impossible for Him.**

The peace that permeated the small room, the power of prayer that flowed and the joy that I knew was on the face of Jesus and the angels as they joined with us already knowing the outcome. Yes, there were tears, but faith rose as we trusted our God who was with us also in the operating room touching the hands of the surgeons working on Garry who was the son of the King.

Earlier than expected, the operating doors opened and out came the professor, still dressed in his scrubs. "I don't believe in God or prayer, but whatever you are doing I encourage you to keep doing. What was clearly on the MRI was no longer evident as I operated. I didn't need to take half of Garry's face, all I did was mop up." he continued, "I've got to say I saw a miracle tonight before my eyes."

Cheers and praise rang through the corridors of the hospital that night as we lifted the mighty name of Jesus high. Praise to our God who chose to be faithful to a family who purposefully knew that Jesus was the master miracle worker.

The next time Dr. Breezy entered the room, he had no words. Like the professor, he just said, "I can't even begin to understand what has just happened." I just reminded him of my words a couple of days before, "You have no idea who our God is and what He can do."

This is one of the many miracles we saw during Garry's time in hospital, and I cannot wait to share other awesome miracles in another chapter as I continue to stand in awe of our God. As I often say, *"I hope I never lose the wonder, the wonder of His mercy."* (Taken from the song written by Matt Redman.)[5]

Nine months later, Garry did go running into the arms of Jesus healthy and whole. As I mentioned earlier, Garry's greatest desire was sharing the love of Jesus with his grandchildren, telling them the stories of the great men and women in the Bible. To honour his desire, as a Nanna, I have chosen, on 27th September each year, to purchase each of my grandchildren something that will encourage them in their walk with Jesus.

God's speciality is to use ordinary people

Stretch out Your hand of power through us to heal, and to move in signs and wonders by the name your holy Son Jesus!

Acts 4:30 (TPT)

The verse that heads this chapter is a prayer I want imprinted on my spirit.

The reason this verse leaps out at me is because Peter and John and the early believers were ordinary people, just like you and me. After meeting or hearing about Jesus, these ordinary people were never the same. They were changed, and their powerful faith and prayers shook the house in which they were meeting.

Peter and John, Unschooled Ordinary Men

This passage in Acts 4:1-35 sends warm fuzzies of power rampantly through my body, not in a negative or crazy way, but enthusiastically unleashing a truth of awe and power.

Peter and John were arrested because they had healed a crippled beggar as they entered the temple at the Gate Beautiful. Not only was the beggar healed, but the apostles also took the opportunity to share with all who would listen. They declared it was not by their power that the cripple was healed, but by the mighty power of Jesus of Nazareth whom they had killed but who had risen and was now in heaven with His Father.

What a difference it will make to us when we have an encounter with Jesus. Just as Peter and John showed a boldness, we too have been given that same power as was given to them. We too can speak out boldly and not be afraid, asking for a power to be unleashed as we pray believing. The leaders saw changed lives, not just ordinary fishermen.

When they saw the courage of Peter and John and realized that they were unschooled, ordinary men, they were astonished and they took note that these men had been with Jesus.
Acts 4:13

What an encouragement to us — As we spend time with Jesus, people will notice. We will be different; we will walk in power and pray that same prayer that was prayed in Acts 4:30. I believe it will delight Jesus to hear us pray, show your mighty power to heal people and work miracles and wonders in the name of your holy Servant Jesus.

These apostles and followers of Jesus were not afraid of the consequences, which were prison and persecution, but they spoke with power. Their prayer was not spoken timidly, asking God to shield them in these dangerous times, rather they boldly spoke out: "... *Lord, give us thy grace to go on steadfastly in our work, and not fear the face of man.*" (As is written in Matthew Henry's commentary). These believers, in faith, prayed this powerful prayer with a heart abandoned to Jesus: "*After they prayed, the place where they were meeting was shaken. And they were all filled with the Holy Spirit and spoke the word of God boldly.*" *Acts 4:31*

What power fills us when we realise who Jesus is, the meaning of the Cross the resurrection and the filling of the Holy Spirit.

A story was shared of two pastors talking to each other. One said, "I don't understand why your church sees so much answered prayer and miracles. My people love God passionately, yet we don't experience the power of God." The other pastor went on to say, "My friend, your church knows the Word of God, but my church lives the Word of God."

I believe that we can live daily in the mighty power of the Holy Spirit. Do we mess up at times? Absolutely, God doesn't mind because He sees our hearts, our intentions, our desires. What we mess up, He wipes up.

An Ordinary Nurse

My gorgeous husband Garry was lying motionless in his room in the transplant unit of the Wesley Hospital when a beautiful young nurse whom we had never met entered the room. With a look of alarm on her face as she observed the numerous machines and tubes attached to his body said, "Oh my goodness, I don't know where to start." I admit her remark certainly did not give me any confidence. I made my way to the nurse's desk to express my concern. With a smile, the head nurse came to oversee things. We came to love and appreciate this delightful young nurse whom I will name Suhana. This beautiful girl did everything with excellence as she made Garry comfortable.

It was early 2009 just after Christmas when she entered Garry's room late one night to see if he was awake. Suhana said, almost in a whisper, "Are we able to talk? I am Indian, as you would know. My husband and I follow the Hindu faith, but I have never experienced a family like yours. Each one displays so much peace, joy, love and confidence in the God that you trust, even with what you are going through. I have observed, when you all pray, answers come. Are you able to share with me what you have that we do not?"

What a bold powerful statement Suhana said that night. Garry, in his hospital bed, sensitively shared Jesus with Suhana. The next morning, Garry excitedly shared what had happened during that night shift. After talking together, we chose to buy the DVD of Jesus for the nurse who was hungry to know truth. We both laid our hands on the

DVD, praying that the words would bring revelation, understanding, breakthrough and real knowledge of Jesus.

As we gave the gift to Suhana, tears trickled down her face and we knew the Holy Spirit was working, bringing a softness and openness to her spirit. On Suhana's next shift, she told us she had not yet watched the DVD as her husband had asked, "Please wait one more night so I can watch it with you. I want to know about this Jesus that Garry has been sharing with you." It did not stop there. Suhana had shared with her neighbours who also asked, "Please, are we also able to see this movie?" What an outcome from one late night conversation.

Garry never saw Suhana again as she was transferred to another ward and Garry was released from hospital. What a God encounter — An ordinary Hindu Indian nurse had been used to spread God's word, just through her passion to know Jesus.

An Ordinary Man About to Die

Richard leaned heavily on the nurse's desk close to Garry's room, very sick and weak. Garry had never seen this man before but asked, "Would you like to have a chat in the lounge just down the hall?" Pale and extremely unwell, he said, "My name is Richard and yes, anything would be better than trying to hobble around these corridors or lying-in bed in pain. My oncologist has just given me some difficult news. I have only two weeks." What an opportunity, Garry thought. He said, "Am I able to pray for you?"

Richard went on to say, "I went to church many years ago but chose to give it away as it meant nothing to me. Now that I'm about to die, I do not want to come crawling back to God. It just doesn't seem right." With a respectful smile, Garry said, "Why not? It is a great time to come running to Jesus. If you were drowning and someone threw a life ring, would you just let it float by? Richard, you would grab hold of it and allow the life ring to bring you to safety and I know you would be very thankful. This is no different. God is saying, Richard, here I am, call out to me, I am your life ring, I am your Saviour."

Joy, peace and comfort filled the tiny room that afternoon as two incredibly sick men shared about a God who was able. With tears flowing, Richard repented and gave his life to Jesus, now ready to enter heaven a brand-new child of God.

Oh, the joy of another person snatched from the clutches of Satan in those last moments.

"Do you have anything I can read? I have no Christian literature and I would love to spend my last days reading and being comforted by Jesus who has accepted me back. Garry, never have I felt like this, ever!"

At home that night, I rummaged through what I thought would be easy reading. I found some Joyce Meyer magazines and took them to the hospital the next day, knowing Richard would find comfort in the words of this mighty woman of God.

Arriving at the hospital, Garry said in a saddened tone, "I haven't seen Richard since our talk. I have looked but I don't know which room he's in." So together, holding each other's hands, in faith we prayed. We asked that Garry would cross paths with Richard one more time to encourage him as he had chosen to trust again. As we prayed, we felt the Holy Spirit challenge us to pray for his healing. It was also our desire this time for him to know God as his loving caring Father, not the God that he had known years before. A God who not only loved but healed and gave a second chance. Oh, the faith that was released that moment. Yes, God was faithful, and Garry had a brief opportunity to pass on the books, encourage and pray once again with Richard.

Two months later, Garry had an appointment with his oncologist. He could hardly walk and needed a wheelchair as his body was weak, so different from his normal well-maintained form. I often smiled when even his sons envied the awesome physique that would ripple with muscle. My man's body may have been frail, but our faith was strong and fervent. As Garry waited to be called, a man walked in robust, healthy and fit. As we locked eyes, we simultaneously recognised each other.

Richard, with a radiant face, excitedly said, "I'm a walking miracle." No longer having only two weeks to live, he had been completely healed, and he knew this was a gift from God. He had become involved in a great church and was living the life that God had destined for him. He was praising God from every fibre of his being. Richard had prayed that he would see us once more to let us know of his healing. He had now come to know a miracle working God, a God who was merciful and full of grace, a powerful God, a God of second chances.

As we celebrated with Richard, that same day, Garry received the news there was nothing more that could be done for him.

"You are our everything, Daddy God," we voiced, and we trust you with our future."

Ordinary Ladies

They were a group of ordinary Life Group ladies – like a smorgasbord, as I often called them. They had such diverse personalities and cultural backgrounds, with each at a different stage in their faith walk but sharing the same immense and awesome love for God and His Word. This group's passion to see God move was unstoppable. They were like the early believers, desiring and hungry to see God's power.

These women had one thing in common – a hunger and love for God, desiring to see His presence and power at work in their lives, and in the lives of others in need.

Meeting each fortnight to study God's word, encourage, love and support each other truly was a gift. At various times during the year, we would have days of prayer and fasting, then at night we would meet to celebrate with praise and worship and God's presence would fall. I still laugh as I recall Tracy coming a little late one night. The door was locked but this did not stop her. We heard her banging on the door above our worship, calling out, "I am hungry for God!"

At our prayer, fasting and worship nights, this group prayed with expectation, choosing to believe nothing was impossible for our God in their requests. Moses expressed he was standing on holy ground as he knelt before the burning bush. There were many times when this Life Group met together, the presence of God was so great that it felt we too were standing on holy ground.

I cannot put a date on when our prayers started to be answered powerfully, continuously and miraculously, but it happened. We started to experience instant healings; addictions and bondages were broken; supernatural answers in finance, employment, family relationships were restored; and miracles became normal. Every week, answers to prayers flowed and God's name was lifted high. I do not believe there were any prayers in that period that went unanswered. God's Spirit flowed. At the conclusion of many meetings, the women were unable to move due to the powerful presence and out pouring of the Holy Spirit.

I wanted to continue building the faith in these ordinary women whose eyes were being opened to a God who was able to do the unthinkable. I chose to light a candle for every prayer that had been answered in this season. One night, 70 candles were flickering. What a sight it was, a tangible recognition of what God was doing. It truly looked like the Catholic Church, and I say this respectfully, and these were only the answers I could remember.

One night, when we opened the door as the ladies were leaving, there was a thick fog that enveloped each car. It sparkled as if there were thousands of diamonds present in the fog. Never had we seen a sight like this before. This diamond infested fog followed each woman home that night. The fog was not present around their neighbourhood or in the side streets. To this day, I believe it was the tangible presence of the Holy Spirit that night, an amazing and undeniable sight never seen before.

Whoever is Willing, God Will Use

The house where Peter, John and the early believers were praying was shaken by the power of the Holy Spirit.

Suhana, the beautiful nurse, her family and neighbours had the privilege of watching the DVD of Jesus and the change he can make in their lives when they came to trust him.

Through Richard's experience, we saw God's amazing grace of healing a man who had walked away from His love but who chose in faith to come back and received a miracle as a result.

This ladies Life Group who saw their many prayers supernaturally answered and encountered a diamond infested fog which I believe was the tangible presence of the Holy Spirit.

God uses ordinary people to do extraordinary tasks, all for His glory and a faith builder for us. He is the God who is over all, but He loves knowing your hearts are in love with Him.

Whether you have a mustard seed of faith, or have been given a gift of unbridled faith, to God it is irrelevant. He uses whatever we are willing to give to Him.

Our wonderful God just wants ordinary people to be sold out for him. He will use his power in signs and wonders to change our cicumstances.

I am trusting You without understanding

"For my thoughts are not your thoughts, neither are your ways my ways," declares the LORD. "As the heavens are higher than the earth, so are my ways higher than your ways and my thoughts than your thoughts."

Isaiah 55:8-9

Words that often tumble from our mouths are, Father God I need and desire healing, a path that will bring a calm in my storm, for my family to know you, why is all this happening to me, where are you God, and so many more heartfelt pleas. Yes Jesus, I will praise You when these answers come to pass, but are we willing to still praise when circumstances are not answered immediately or as we had planned, thought, believed or desired?

We have become a society that wants answers as soon as we ask, and if they are not forthcoming immediately, we are sometimes told our faith is not strong enough, there is sin in our lives or you need to pray more. At these times discouragement creeps in and we are prone to believe the lies the evil one feeds us.

Let's look at what Ephesians 6 is asking. Paul is saying to be in strong in the Lord and in His mighty power. It also says to put on the whole armour of God so that you can stand against the devil's schemes, for our struggle is not against flesh and blood but against the powers of this dark world and the spiritual forces of evil in heavenly realms.

Again, this passage asks us to put on the full armour of God so we can take ground. If our answers have not come then this great apostle continues to say, *and after you have done everything, to stand.* Many times, we fail to dress ready for the fight and I visualize the enemy laughing as we go out to fight our battles in blue jeans and T-shirts, with no authority, no armour and no assurance that God will fight for us. Hence, we are defeated and fail to understand why there is no victory.

If we reach for our armour, I hope it is not spotless as if it has been tucked away in our top drawer, protected with moth balls and our socks to keep it from being scratched. I would love it to have many dents, arrow marks and dirt so the evil one will shudder at the sight of it and say, "This one is not for me; as they know how to fight," and will flee without taking a second look.

Paul knew what it was like to fight battles in the heavenlies, and his answer did not always come quickly. This mighty apostle stood, pleading with God three times to be free from the thorn in his flesh. At last, his answer came, but not in the way he had hoped or yearned. This was his answer from God whom he loved, followed, trusted and was ready to give his life for —

But he said to me, "My grace is sufficient for you,
for my power is made perfect in weakness."
2 Corinthians 12:9a

He then went on to say after not being given the words he longed to hear:

Therefore I will boast all the more gladly about my
weaknesses, so that Christ's power may rest on me.
2 Corinthians 12:9b

Can we say that Paul did not have enough faith as the thorn was not taken away? Of course not, but he did receive his answer and he was content in the answer given because he went on to say in the following verse —

That is why, for Christ's sake, I delight in weaknesses,
in insults, in hardships, in persecutions, in difficulties.

For when I am weak, then I am strong.
2 Corinthians 12:10

• • • • • • •

From the moment Garry was diagnosed with this rare, insidious, aggressive strand of leukaemia we chose to speak out God's word as I have written earlier, not looking to the right or the left, but directly into the eyes of Jesus who was to be Garry's healer. We also chose to have communion every day and spent time praising, knowing that Jesus had gone to the cross to heal all diseases.

Praise the LORD, O my soul; all my inmost being, praise his holy name. Praise the LORD, O my soul, and forget not all His benefits – who forgives all your sins and heals all your diseases, who redeems with love and compassion,
Psalms 103:1-4

As Garry's condition worsened, our faith grew stronger, knowing God was above all illnesses. We stood resolutely for his healing. The enemy saw this as an opportunity to inflict barbs, hoping that our faith would revert to scepticism. Our armour however was firmly in place.

One night, around 8.00pm, Garry received a phone call from a Christian man whilst I held a bowl close by as he was continually feeling nauseous due to the side effects of chemotherapy. "Garry, I believe you are encountering this sickness due to the sins in your life."

My humble man, even in his weakened condition listened to this gentleman then graciously said, "I would prefer you not to call me again," and returned the phone to me.

In every healing that is recorded in the gospels, Jesus never brought negative and hurtful words whilst people were at their lowest. In love, compassion and mercy he always brought words of comfort, tenderness, wisdom and healing. The evil one delights in bringing words of discouragement, despair and ugliness, wanting to perpetuate an already difficult situation.

These words came from the pit of hell. Oh, the preciousness of God – the next afternoon I believe I was escorted I would like to think by Michael, the Archangel (maybe not Michael but with assurance of an angelic being), to Word Christian Book Shop. What an honour it is to be a daughter of the King. I was miraculously led through the aisles until I stood in front of a book written by Joseph Prince, 'Destined to Reign'. I had not read a book by this author. This book miraculously opened, and my eyes fell on the words written on pg. 71:

"Have you been fed this lie before? Have you been told that the negative things that you may be experiencing are a result of God's discipline because of your sins? My friend, this is utter nonsense and utter cruelty. God does not punish sin in the new covenant with sicknesses and diseases because sin has already been punished on the body of Jesus. His blood has already been shed for the forgiveness of all our sins. When you received Jesus Christ into your life, all your sins were washed away. It is a finished work." [6]

God had spoken to me ever so personally and miraculously. I bought this book then drove back to the hospital to share God's goodness with Garry. Through this humbling intimacy I had just encountered, I took the time that night to think on what had brought us to this point in our lives. My God had become my dearest and closest friend. I truly believed He could do anything in the natural and the supernatural.

• • • • • • •

Allow me to briefly reflect on how God had brought Garry and I together and led us to this moment in our lives.

As a teenager I remember my mum saying, "Lynn, you can't keep doing this. Aren't any of these guys you have dated worth a long-term relationship?" I would run outside our front gate so my mum could say without lying to the guy who was calling, "I'm sorry, Lynette is not home at the moment" and then I would return inside.

Yes, they were great guys, yes, they were fun, generous, attentive and Christian, but they were just not for me. I answered her question, "Mum, I would rather be single for the rest of my life. I only want God's choice."

I did want my husband to be fun, cheeky and adventurous, to make me laugh and accept me for who I was, to love my family and have a heart that was kind and showed kindness. Also, my passion was to have a husband who was sold out to Jesus, a man who treated me with honour and respect, one with whom together we could take everything to God in prayer. I longed for a man who desired to seek God's answers before those of our flesh, a man whose heart hungered after God and His ways.

I worked with Wendy, and we became friends. She knew I was a Christian, and that was all she needed to know "Lynn, would you like to come to my place for dinner on Friday night?" Not knowing her intentions, I said, "Absolutely, I would like that." Little did I know that Wendy's reason for inviting me home was to meet her brother, who was too shy at the time to ask a girl out, so this scheming little sister chose to step in.

Garry, a thoughtful young man who had a passion and hunger for God, was a singer in a much sought after popular Christian country group. He also possessed all my other desired attributes and most of all, had also been praying for God's choice of a wife. Two years later, this young man with whom I had fallen in love, met me at the end of the aisle, where we knew our wonderful God had brought us together. Love in abundance was unleashed as we were married.

Through 42 treasured years, we shared our lives. Our marriage was filled with laughter, adventure, craziness, children, travel and ministering together. It was an assortment of love and life, always with God at the helm. Through the great and challenging times, we sought God and hungered after Him and His guidance in each decision. We experienced tough times and saw the miraculous, and through it all we loved each other more than life itself.

· · · · · · ·

We were now at this moment being confronted with the greatest challenge of our married life. We listened as the words of Garry's knowledgeable haematologist echoed in the room: "I'm so sorry, there is nothing more we can do." My treasured frail man replied as he extended his hand in gratitude, "Dr. Bashford, I want to thank you for all you have done for me. Please don't be sorry or disappointed. You have truly done your best in the medical realm. You have given me of yourself, and all that medicine is able to do. You have freely given more than just a doctor, you have shared with me your heart and emotions, and I thank you. Now I want you to see what my God will continue to do."

As we returned to the car we both allowed our emotions the freedom to flow, and we sobbed as we held each other tightly. Arriving home, we did as was our practice. Kneeling on the floor and holding each other's hands, we shared with our loving and faithful Heavenly Father: "Man has done all they can, our lives continue to be in Your hands, whatever that may mean." Again, as on other occasions, we handed this monumental difficulty to God and trusted Him with the outcome. Again, we asked for God's healing, and we trusted and rested in the peace that was ours.

God will never let us down. In the natural it may have seemed that way, and I would have loved things to have been different. The words of the Prophet Isaiah 55:8-9 that God's ways were different to ours brought us peace as we walked with Him, loved Him and He loved us in return. Our love relationship with our ever-faithful God brought trust and intimacy that united us even closer.

When God chose to take Garry to his heavenly home, there would have been much cheering as he received his great reward. The accolades would have surprised this incredibly humble beautiful man.

Garry's joy of entering heaven was so different to what lay ahead for me. We had only been in Brisbane two weeks when this journey began for us. Most of Garry's time when he was ill was spent at the Wesley Hospital. My loss was great. I had some family, but no friends, no job, no life and no church to call home. I would go to bed each night clutching my Bible as this was the closest I could be to God. Each day, unable to pray in my own words, I would say The Lord's Prayer. My grief was immense and I remember saying to my daughter-in-law's father, Barry, who was a pastor in Sydney, after the funeral, "Barry, I just want to go to be with Garry." I had lost my soulmate and treasured husband. My dreams were shattered, and I was living in a city unfamiliar to me. The man I loved so much was no longer my earthly rock. I felt so alone, with very little support — but in my grief this verse rang in my ears.

And I am convinced that nothing can ever separate us from God's love. Neither death nor life, neither angels nor demons, neither our fears for today nor our worries about tomorrow – not even the powers of hell can separate us from God's love. No power in the sky above or in the earth below – indeed, nothing in all creation will ever be able to separate us from the love of God that is revealed in Christ Jesus our Lord.

Romans 8:38-39 NLT

I can still hear His words clearly, "Lynn, my work in and through you is not complete."

Through all we encountered, we trusted God implicitly as we daily took communion whilst declaring His promises. Our faith always rose to the heights not allowing doubts to linger in our thoughts. Ultimately, we bowed to the path that God mapped out for us and His purposes, that at the time we did not understand, even as Garry went to his heavenly home.

Without my treasured Garry, God has been faithful, when circumstances have been good or in those difficult times, God, through the Holy Spirit has been my comfort, my strength and all I have needed. His joy is like a well within my spirit, rising and flowing out like lava from a volcano. His purposes are yet to be completed in my life. What an honour and a privilege of loving and serving such an intimate God.

... for the joy of the LORD is your strength.
Nehemiah 8:10

I have walked many paths in life that I have not understood,
but these words would continually spring from my heart:
I may not always understand You Father God, I may
not always understand Your Word or Your ways,
but yet will I love you, yet will I trust you, and yet
will I lift you up as my great and mighty God.

Satan is powerless when we know who we are in Christ

No, in all these things we are more than conquerors through him who loved us.
Romans 8:37

- Oh, the power of prayer
- Oh, the excitement when we pray and faith rises
- Not just drips, Jesus, but a waterfall of answered prayer

As I write this chapter, tears well up as I reflect in gratitude to my God for the countless number of answered prayers that flood my being. I want to dance and sing. No matter what the battle or difficulty — He is able, and He is always and forever faithful.

Often, as Christians, when we face struggles, we allow ourselves to be consumed by the situation, but the Holy Spirit whispers or sometimes calls out loud — Rise up, even if you need friends to hold up your hands while the battle rages as was the case for Moses (Exodus 17), when we can't do it alone, have people stand with you supporting you — Rise up, we have the capacity to be conquerors!

… if God is for us, who can be against us?
Romans 8:31

While we were living in Jakarta, our son Peter was cursed with a powerful spirit of fear with which he had been cursed by a *dukun* (Indonesian for witch doctor). This came about when we needed to dismiss one of our house staff. Often, the practice is, if a person has been dismissed from employment, with their final wages, they would go to the *dukun* and have a curse placed on the most vulnerable member of the household.

This fear crippled Peter and left him powerless to live life as he had known. We had never been confronted with such a curse. Prior to this demonic encounter, Peter was an outgoing, funny, charismatic, charming, engaging ten-year old. Teachers, friends and anyone who met Peter loved being with our vivacious son.

Garry and I had not been familiar with spirits, curses and supernatural powers of this nature, so this was unchartered waters for us. Now, living in Jakarta, we had a front row seat experiencing the powers of the satanic and the strength of this spirit.

We prayed and did what we could as we watched our gorgeous son clinging to the column in our house daily, sobbing, "Please do not take me to school." Peter had previously loved school due to the many opportunities for mischief to be his close friend.

How faithful our God was at this difficult time. As we prayed, Peter was given a Christian teacher in Grade 5, then in year 6, fear overwhelmed him at the possibility of being in a classroom that overlooked the local graveyard. Prayer again being our powerful weapon, we shared with our treasured boy, even being ten, God really cared. With no parental intervention, Peter was placed in the classroom that overlooked the beautifully maintained gardens at the school, again he experienced God's amazing faithfulness.

During these years, Peter was imprisoned unable to sleep in his own room, unable to attend birthday parties unless Garry or I were present or live the vibrant life that he had loved. We prayed and asked others to pray but we were unable to break this insidious power that held him captive.

God is always ready to give an encouragement when we have eyes to see. I was given a book to read, 'Like Lambs to the Slaughter' by Johanna Michaelsen, which gave me the assurance that this foul curse could be broken, and Peter set free. At the time, the occult was rarely talked about, especially within Christian circles. On one home leave, we took Peter for prayer. The picture was given that he was like a butterfly trapped in a net where specific and specialised instruments were needed to sever the threads that were unusually strong to set Peter free.

Due to our growing experience and knowledge of evil powers, we were asked to be involved in the deliverance of a young American girl that had been cursed by her friends. This manifested in the form of eyes that were in a picture that hung on her bedroom wall which followed her every move. What a time of deliverance we experienced that night as we commanded this spirit to leave. Oh, the power that is in the name of Jesus, as this spirit fled, screaming as we applied the precious blood of Jesus.

Again, I was involved in a small group and given the privilege whilst in Jakarta to come to pray for Lucy. This beautiful 12-year-old Dutch girl was unable to walk, and like Peter, had been cursed and was now relegated to a wheelchair. As prayer and praise filled the room, Lucy experienced the paralysis leave, and healing come strengthening her legs until she excitedly said, "Mum, can I get out of my wheelchair?" *God's power to deliver and heal is undeniable.*

While seeing many others set free, our own Peter was still held captive, but God's faithfulness did not disappoint as we stood firm. We were still holding resolutely to our belief when our four-year secondment to Indonesia came to an end.

Being led by the Holy Spirit, we became aware that one of my Baptist Sunday school teachers of many years' past was ministering in deliverance. We contacted this godly couple, knowing we could trust them implicitly and with the assurance our answer through Jesus was at hand. A time was set for our treasured son to experience his freedom.

What a night it was! Garry and I knelt in prayer as this couple were used by God to set Peter free to now reach his destiny in Jesus. The bondage of this insidious fear was broken and this filthy, foul spirit was gone forever and freedom was now his after four years of torment. His face glowed and we all knew victory had conquered.

This beautiful older couple wisely said, "Peter, you have had spiritual surgery tonight, and this sinister and unusually strong evil spirit of fear has been cast out, and the door tightly shut. We have prayed God's amazing gifts to replace what has departed. Peter, this type of spirit still revels in lurking around, speaking lies to your mind as it has done for the past four years." They continued, "Precious young man, you must stand up and let them know that Jesus is now master of your mind. Let these demonic voices know you have been set free by the mighty power that is in the name of Jesus." I chose to write verses that would empower Pete to speak out and declare what had been done that night of spiritual surgery. Two of those powerful verses that would quieten the voices and render them powerless.

For God has not given us a spirit of fear and timidity,
but of power, love, and self-discipline.
2 Timothy 1:7 NLT

----- All power is given unto me in heaven and in earth.
Matthew 28:18

Every day, as Peter dressed for school, he would choose a verse and place it in his shirt pocket, and whenever a thought would start to emerge, he immediately reached for that verse and read it out boldly, declaring his freedom in Jesus. For nine months, Peter confidently spoke out God's word, even asking his teacher if necessary could he leave the classroom to use the bathroom so he could read aloud. For nine months, he fought the enemy's voices, taking his spiritual medicine continually and proclaiming God's word. Nine months, he lived and breathed the word of God.

During those nine months, the voices became softer and less frequent, but Peter never stopped declaring these verses until every voice bowed to the name of Jesus.

The enemy was crushed, Peter was set free, never again to be inflicted with thoughts of fear, never again afraid. That night, when this Godly couple broke the curse over Peter, they prayed God's gifts into him. Immediately after that night, the gifts of discernment, knowledge and wisdom became evident as they manifest to this day.

Peter became a mighty teenager for God, knowing that what God's word says would always come to be. Today, he helps and challenges others to speak out and live God's word, knowing there will always be victory.

Off Limits, Satan

Every day, whilst my treasured Garry was in the Wesley Hospital, we knew God's presence filled his room as this was His gift to us.

As I wrote in the previous chapter, we had purchased a small sound system and saturated Garry's room continually with God's word and praise. There was to be no room for the evil one to use this situation as their playground of fear and negativity.

The presence of God was powerful even in the inconceivable severity of the situation. Praise was being sung quietly in the background continually day and night as the nurses and doctors did what was necessary and peace reigned.

How could you not smile as you entered his room? Garry loved his assortment of fluorescent t-shirts and the doctors delighted in this distraction from the gloom of illness and death by taking stakes as to which colour would be worn each day.

Garry was loved by the staff, from the cleaner to the specialist. No matter how he was feeling, he always put others first, caring and giving words of encouragement or sharing a joke with anyone who entered.

But this one morning was different. Sensing something was amiss, I asked, "Garry, are you okay?" "Princess, last night was one I don't ever want to encounter again." Perplexed, I asked, "Why?" Garry, replied, "It was around 3.00am and I woke to see absolutely grotesque, evil, obnoxious figures at my door. Lynn, they were demons, each fighting to gain entry. Unable to succeed, they became even more agitated. It was an horrific sight; one I had never encountered and never want to experience again. I wasn't afraid just sickened and I reached out and turned the volume louder on my CD player so praise would cause each demon to lose its power. I then closed my eyes, taking authority over this demonic activity."

Thank you Father God for the power of Your word and the gift of praise. These demons who tried to take advantage of a man who was sick and vulnerable lost their fight because the presence of God filled his room. They became aware that they were powerless to enter.

Garry and I knew the power of our extraordinary God and the power that is in the name of Jesus. These demons had to succumb to the realisation they were no match to the presence of God as they scurried away with the blood of Jesus chasing them. Oh, the sight it must have been for those who had the spiritual eyes to see.

Dancing to Freedom

My friend Christine and I had the privilege of praying for a young lady who came for prayer. Suzie wanted victory in her situation as she had arrived in Australia and after some months was unable to secure a job.

We knew that our wonderful God cares about every detail of those who love and trust Him implicitly. So, coming together for prayer was such a natural thing. We delighted in this ministry, knowing there was victory in every circumstance we brought to Him.

After a time of prayer, faith rose and with the knowledge that God had heard our prayer, Suzie excitedly said, "I want to dance!" As the music played, my lounge room enjoyed the activity of three ladies dancing as praise rang out, assuring that victory was now Suzie's.

Due to past encounters, Suzie wanted to be armed with all God had for her but was a little concerned. What if the faith now within her was snatched away and disappointment and discouragement returned as had happened previously?

I encouraged Suzie to choose to rise above her natural feelings of concern by doing something in the physical. It must have made God laugh as three grown women stood on chairs as a symbol of being above any negativity, and to encourage Suzie to believe that she could fly with eagles in faith as God's promises were unleashed.

Suzie diligently continued this practice, not giving the enemy a foothold in her search for jobs. Every day, she would stand on the chair and declare God's word over her soon-to-be employment.

Eventually, Suzie was successful in her search and attained a position with a high-profile company. To this day, as we talk over coffee, Suzie radiates, sharing that her promotions have come in ways that in the natural seemed impossible.

Suzie's chair may be an encouragement for those facing hardship. Let us be proactive and show the enemy that we fly with the eagles, speaking God's promises and not succumbing to disappointment or scratching below in the territory of disillusionment and defeat.

We are overcomers when our eyes are fixed on him

A Purified Church

An insidious sin infiltrated the church I was attending. This sin was starting to affect marriages and families, bringing shame and dishonour to beautiful Godly people. However, not all members were aware of what was taking place.

As I became aware of this situation, I put on my spiritual boxing gloves and let the evil one be aware he is messing with the wrong lady. I knew my place in Christ and Satan's time was now over as he inflicted his ugliness of sin on these families, causing potential destruction to God's church.

The power and victory that awaits us when we know who we are in christ, and He will fight for us

After speaking to my pastor at the time of what I had become aware, I left his office disheartened, dispirited and angry. Nothing was going to be done because one of those involved held much influence in this church. "How can this be?" I cried out to God. "Lynn, my Son Jesus has felt as you feel, but you know the answer is in me," came His reply.

Knowing that I had heard directly from my God, I spoke out these words confidently and aggressively, "Satan, you will not bring the Bride of Christ into disrepute, and you will not win. Victory and power belong to those who love and walk in the knowledge of the King of Kings."

Coming home from work each day, I donned my joggers and sweats and walked my daily ten kilometres. The first five kilometres, I would sing, knowing that praise paralyses Satan, and for the next five, I would cry out and intercede, condemning the cruel work of the enemy. Day after day, kilometre after kilometre, my aching heart would call out to God in intercession as tears ran down my face. God do not let the evil one gain victory in your church and in these beautiful marriages. I never spoke to the pastor again on this issue, I just allowed God to do His work as this was His church. Our wonderful faithful God heard my cries of intercession and intervened. Not long after the pastor left, and a spirit filled young man came, bringing healing and restoration.

This church is now a light in every part of their community, bringing health, wholeness, liberty and care to thousands. Whatever the need, this church reaches out. God has restored what the evil one sought to steal and destroy.

For the Lord your God is the one who goes with you to fight for you against your enemies to give you victory.
Deuteronomy 20:4

God, who is over all, has given to us the assurance through His word that He will overcome everything the enemy puts in our way. I encourage you to take hold of His promises. Live, breathe and speak out God's word with boldness, not giving the evil one an inkling or indication that he can win.

I encourage you to take God's word, choose to believe it, live it, walk in it, even if circumstances say there is no hope.

In our wonderful God, there is always hope and victory

No foothold for you Satan

… and do not give the devil a foothold.
Ephesians 4:27

At times, I have been guilty of running to people before running to God, asking for wisdom when my spirit has been wounded. Our faithful God says, come to me, all the help you need is in My Word.

My help comes from the LORD, the Maker of heaven and earth.
Psalms 121:2

God is our refuge and strength, an ever-present help in trouble.
Psalms 46:1

Whilst on holidays and a long way from home, in an out-of-the-blue moment, someone spoke harshly to me which caught me off guard. I went to my room and knelt beside my bed and said, "God, I feel so hurt." My heart was still tender and raw due to my Garry not being with me, and I did not want to stay. At first, I let my flesh take over and I sent an email to my daughter. Without saying what had transpired, I wrote, "Kylie, would you please pray for me?" and that is all that was written. Next, I wrote an email to someone whom I knew had much Godly wisdom, asking for advice but did not press the 'send' key. I left my email sitting on my computer.

Feeling offended, I cried out to my closest friend. "Father God, I need Your guidance in this situation. What should I do?" Then I listened. In no time, these words came to me. "Lynn, go to my Word." I laughed and said, "Your Word is very large with many books?" Equally,

I saw His smile, "Lynn, go to Philippians." I picked up my Bible and turned to this book and chose to start reading from the beginning. Yes, there was my answer in verse 27. It was as if Jesus was standing right beside me.

Whatever happens, conduct yourselves in a
manner worthy of the gospel of Christ.
Philippians 1:27a.

Even though there was no 'Oh, poor Lynnie, I see your pain', I knew Jesus could see my heart. The verse that had been given was so apt for what I had asked. I absolutely delighted in God's wisdom through His word; I was excited at the His amazing intimacy. I knew the words had come quickly and directly from God's mouth through Paul's teaching. No longer did I need the words of man, so I deleted the email as I had heard unmistakeably from my loving Heavenly Father.

Often, we seek man over God and His word, but He is willing to speak if we are prepared to seek, listen and obey what has been given. As I chose God's word, He lovingly touched and healed my wounded heart. What a privilege to experience one of God's priceless and intimate encounters. Yes, I was able to put this verse into practice with the encouragement and strength of the Holy Spirit.

A wounded spirit can be used so powerfully by the enemy. I so want to encourage you as it says in God's word, "*and do not give the devil a foothold." Ephesians 4:27.*

You may be saying, "Lynn, my hurt is so much deeper than what you have shared of your wounded spirit." You may have been betrayed, made a mistake and judged for it, or wounded in a myriad of ways. But our wonderful God is there, willing to listen and to guide. He may use His word as He did for me. He may use a trusted friend's listening ear and wise words or a counsellor, but what I want you to know is He is there, ready to shower you with His wisdom, compassion, mercy and grace.

One morning, I woke up around 4.00am. Not able to go back to sleep, I turned on my television to hear the words powerfully spoken by Joyce Meyer resounding in a stadium filled to capacity. "What a difference we could make in this world if we as Christians could be quick to forgive."

He heals the broken-hearted and binds up their wounds.
Psalms 147:3

Will you dare to take up the challenge?

Now to him who is able to do
immeasurably more than all we ask or
imagine, according to his power
that is at work within us,
Ephesians 3:20

Sitting in my Life Group at Lugarno Baptist Church many years ago, our leader Rod gave us a challenge: "Are you ready to stand up and make a difference in someone's life?" With the authority in his voice, he had my attention, and I was excited.

He put this challenge to us: "I'm suggesting that each one think of a person and pray Ephesians 3:14-21 into their life for one week and we will talk about it next time we meet." Rod went on to say that these verses are the Apostle Paul's prayer to the Ephesian church. I was eager and ready for this challenge as it brought out my competitive nature and love for prayer. I went home, read this passage through many times, and then prayerfully chose my person.

For this reason I kneel before the Father, from whom his whole family in heaven and on earth derives its name. I pray that out of his glorious riches he may strengthen you with power through his Spirit in your inner being, so that Christ may dwell in your hearts through faith. And I pray that you, being rooted and established in love, may have power, together with all the saints, to grasp how wide and long and high and deep is the love of Christ, and to know this love that surpasses knowledge – that you may be filled to the measure of all the fullness of God. Now to him who is able to do immeasurably more than all we ask or imagine, according to his power that is at work within us, to him be glory in the church and in Christ Jesus throughout all generations, for ever and ever! Amen.

Ephesians 3:14-21

I loved this challenge, and diligently prayed over the person I had selected. After the week, these verses so filled my soul that the passion for speaking out this passage rose within me and would not be quietened. I decided to continue the challenge, but this time praying over my family.

I printed out these verses and together with Garry, we knelt each night, declaring this passage over our children. I was enthusiastic and loved verse 20. *"Now to Him who is able to do immeasurably more than all we ask or imagine, according to His power that is at work with us."* Garry was a little unsure, especially when my enthusiasm rose, and I included the word 'dream'. You see, I believe God wants us to dream big dreams with Him. Yes, to have audacious dreams and a daring faith. Just as we love a challenge, I believe He does also.

As our family grew, so did those we included in our prayers – husbands, wives, our grandchildren, and the generations to come. We were praying in faith and did not want any in our heritage to miss out.

God promises His Word will never return void. We declared the truths spoken in this passage with power, faith and expectancy, looking in anticipation for what God would do. I was sharing this with a friend in Canada, and she said, "Lynn, you have not just prayed this prayer, but you have prophesied these words over your family." I laughed and said, "Gisele, you are so right."

If you are reading this chapter, I would love to inspire and encourage you to also take up this challenge that Rod gave me so long ago. Choose to pray these verses over your families, friends, and those whom God lays in your heart. I pray that excitement will rise within you, as a vision of what God can do as His Word is released and prophesied.

God's word is powerful, God's word brings change, God's word transforms lives, God's word paralyses the enemy.

My encouragement is not to give up but diligently speak out, not giving in to tiredness, apathy or busyness, but trust God for how He will use His words through you.

Rise to the challenge and change our world for God's glory

Heroes God uses to deepen my faith

Joseph -- Daniel -- Rahab

These three heroes of faith chose to look at
God and not at their circumstances.
This also became my choice.

Lynn, in every circumstance like Joseph, Daniel, Rahab and many others mentioned in God's word, you so boldly, confidently, courageously and daringly chose to stand in faith, not giving up. How did you continue to do this in all that you have been through, many have asked.

My answer has always been and will always be as I penned in an earlier chapter: "I may not always understand God, I may not always understand His word or His ways, but yet I will love Him, yet I will trust Him, and yet I will lift Him up as the great and mighty God, no matter what twists and turns come my way."

I remember, as a teenage girl, jumping up each morning to switch on the heater on those cold mornings, hoping back into bed until the bars on the heater glowed. Then, sitting in the warmth as I spent time interacting with God and His Word. Those special times are still indelibly imprinted on my mind – My Daddy God and me.

Whilst still dark each Saturday morning as a teenager, Bob, a young man who also loved God passionately, would call at my place at 5.00am. Together we would walk to the train station and travel a few suburbs for a 6.00am prayer meeting. What powerful times of intercession these were as we met and prayed for those who attended Teen Ranch, a Christian camp site for youth across Sydney and beyond to be impacted for God. I knew at a young age God was my Heavenly Father whom I could trust and was faithful, who loved and cherished me.

I wanted to be His girl as I had been engraved on the palm of His hand, as it says in Isaiah 49:16. I know this was written to Israel, but

Jesus willingly went to the Cross for each one, hence His love for Israel has been extended to us as Gentiles, and I rejoice in these words. My early morning heater dates with God and early morning prayer escapades helped to build a love for my Heavenly Father that has never been extinguished.

My experiences as a teenage girl were not difficult, but I believe loving God and learning of Him were a training ground for what I was to face in future years.

Don't let anyone look down on you because you are young, but set an example for the believers in speech, in life, in love, in faith and in purity.
1 Timothy 4:12

Paul, the writer of 1 Timothy, is not saying only young-in-age but also in faith. What an encouragement; no matter where we stand in life, God says we can be used as an example to all.

God is God in every phase of life. God is God in every circumstance, whether we understand it or not. I ask each one who is reading this book to hold tightly to God's promises, never giving up, and visualise those you pray for rising from the ashes.

"Come to me, all you who are weary and burdened, and I will give you rest. Take my yoke upon you and learn from me, for I am gentle and humble in heart, and you will find rest for your souls. For my yoke is easy and my burden is light."
Matthew 11:28-30

No matter what our occurrences, Jesus gives us hope and rest in our trials. He whispers so lovingly, "You can trust Me, but it is your choice. I will never abandon you. You are my mine." I know this following verse has strong imagery, but it is the heart of God as David writes –

You keep track of all my sorrows. You have collected all my tears in your bottle. You have recorded each one in your book.
Psalms 56:8 NLT

Reading God's word, I find numerous people whom I would call great, all passed through the fires of life. I continue, even now, to encounter those who stand firm as they experience harrowing, unimaginable and unthinkable circumstances, yet they stand resolutely holding onto God and His Word as their spirit finds peace.

When you pass through the waters, I will be with you; and when you pass through the rivers, they will not sweep over you. When you walk through the fire, you will not be burned; the flames will not set you ablaze.
Isaiah 43:2

Each of Jesus' disciples faced horrendous and cruel deaths except for John who was boiled in oil. He escaped only to live out the rest of his days on the Isle of Patmos with unscrupulous characters. It was on this island that he was given the words to the book of Revelation. These disciples would never have endured their deaths had they not seen in Jesus, their leader a man who could be trusted even to death.

In November 1873, Horatio Spafford's four children drowned in a major sea collision. With only his wife surviving, he was able to pen this heartfelt old hymn as he himself sailed over that same sight a couple of weeks later.

"When peace like a river, attendeth my way,
When sorrows like sea billows roll,
Whatever my lot, Thou hast taught me to know,
It is well, it is well with my soul."[7]

In recent times, I have invested much time in reading the life story of Nabeel Qureshi. This young devout Muslim diligently searched for truth for four years whilst rooming with a Christian college student. He came to an exceptional understanding of Jesus. Nabeel, a brilliant author and apologist, has influenced thousands through his writings, speaking and debates. Nabeel, with his unstoppable faith, died of stomach cancer at 34 years, leaving his beautiful wife and two-year old daughter. I cannot begin to understand these circumstances. The Holy Spirit spoke these words, "It is not for you to question why, only trust."

As I reflect on much of what I've read and experienced, God continually reminds me of my many heroes in the bible whom I have come to love as I read their life stories. They have been a great source of encouragement through my challenging times.

Let me start with Joseph.

Joseph, at 17 years of age, was thrown into a pit by his jealous brothers whilst visiting as they were shepherding their father's sheep. In their anger they then dragged him out and sold him into slavery as a camel train passed by and was taken to Egypt. One of Pharaoh's officials named Potiphar bought him as he had eyes to see that the Lord was with this young man. Joseph was placed in charge of Potiphar's household and was entrusted with all that he owned.

What an admirable young man. Joseph, at such a young age, unfairly treated by his brothers, taken from his homeland, now a slave, was still upright, honourable, pure in heart and faultless. As a well-built, handsome young man, he chose not to succumb to the sexual advances of his master's wife, hence she chose to lie about him. Even though honest in all he did, this young Israelite found himself thrown into prison, but it says, "The LORD was with him" (Genesis 39:21).

What encouragement for us when we find ourselves in circumstances not of our own choosing and we wonder, is God still in control?

At God's appointed time, Pharaoh, who was ruler of Egypt, after having a dream, heard that Joseph had a gift of interpretation.

So Pharaoh asked them, "Can we find anyone like this man, one in whom is the spirit of God?" Then Pharaoh said to Joseph, "Since God has made all this known to you, there is no one so discerning and wise as you. You shall be in charge of my palace, and all my people are to submit to your orders. Only with respect to the throne will I be greater than you."

Genesis 41:38-40

As we read this story. we could say, "Where were you, God, when the situation with Joseph was so emphatically unfair."

Can you imagine if that occurred today? There would be emails criss-crossing in cyber space at a rapid rate, copious text messages sent, and phone calls made to the leaders of our nation. Churches would be organising prayer meetings and times of fasting. Let me quickly say that this would not be wrong, but God's perfect plan was set in motion for Joseph, as it is for us in what we face. It was no mistake that Joseph was in prison, and as we continue reading, we see a whole nation being saved from starvation and a family restored.

God's plans are so much higher than our plans and thoughts. Even in prison Joseph was honourable and continued to be God's man in this difficult situation.

"For my thoughts are not your thoughts, neither are your ways my ways," declares the LORD. "As the heavens are higher than the earth, so are my ways higher than your ways and my thoughts than your thoughts."

Isaiah 55:8-9

My next hero is Daniel.

Daniel was also captured at a young age and taken into slavery in Babylon. Daniel's life was exemplary in all ways and he distinguished himself among the administrators and governors of that day. As in the story of Joseph, jealousy came into play, and men of high rank sought ways to take Daniel down in the eyes of the king. However, they were unable to find any corruption in him because he was so trustworthy. (Daniel 6). These wicked, evil men with self-inflated egos devised a plan to rid Daniel from the palace. They asked the king to put into writing a decree that anyone who prayed to any God or human for the following 30 days except for himself to be thrown into the lion's den.

Now when Daniel learned that the decree had been published, he went home to his upstairs room where the windows opened toward Jerusalem. Three times a day he got down on his knees and prayed, giving thanks to his God, just as he had done before."
Daniel 6:10

Again, these devious and ruthless men went as a group to find Daniel who was praying and asking God for help. Without a moment's hesitation, they set off quickly to the king and reported that Daniel was not paying attention and honouring the royal decree that had been given. This news brought much distress upon the King as he respected, valued and appreciated Daniel. He was determined to rescue and save him. Unable to recant on his own given law, Daniel was hurled into the den of lions, the king said, *"May your God, whom you serve continually, rescue you!" (Daniel 6:16)*

At the first light of dawn, the king got up and hurried to the lions' den. When he came near the den, he called to Daniel in an anguished voice, "Daniel, servant of the living God, has your God, whom you serve continually, been able to rescue you from the lions?" Daniel answered, "O king, live forever! My God sent his angel, and he shut the mouths of the lions. They have not hurt me, because I was found innocent in his sight. Nor have I ever done any wrong before you, O king."

Daniel 6:19-22

Justice was served that same day to those who sought to come up against this mighty man of God. Yes, God is our justifier and to understand that the battle always belongs to the Lord.

Then King Darius wrote to all the peoples, nations and men of every language throughout the land: "May you prosper greatly! I issue a decree that in every part of my kingdom people must fear and reverence the God of Daniel. For he is the living God and he endures forever; his kingdom will not be destroyed, his dominion will never end. He rescues and he saves; he performs signs and wonders in the heavens and on the earth. He has rescued Daniel from the power of the lions."

Daniel 6:25-27

Daniel stood firm in adversity, not wavering but trusting his God to be his vindicator. It was as if he put blinkers on and looked into the eyes of his God, not looking to the right or the left, but saying, "I will trust in You no matter what law or decree is given. You are my God; in You I will trust even if it means my life will be snatched away."

Lastly, I would like to talk of Rahab.

Rahab was an amazing woman. Yes, she was a prostitute, maybe not by her own choice, but one that may have been chosen for her. This woman played a significant and vital role in the Israelites coming into the land that God had promised.

After Moses died, Joshua took command of the Israelite people. This time he chose two men to enter the city of Jericho and spy out the land that he, Calab and ten others had done 40 years prior. That first endeavour was met by ten out of the twelve spies returning a report filled with much dread and terror as they looked at their own humanity instead of their awe-inspiring God who had miraculously led them out of Egypt. This exodus exhibited a supernatural opening of the Red Sea, and a protection from the Egyptian army as God used a pillar of fire at night and a cloud that hid them by day. God wanted to lead his people directly into their destiny that He had prepared, but much fear stopped this from occurring. How full of grace and mercy our God is, giving these people a second chance to enter the land that flowed with milk and honey spoken to Moses through the burning bush prior to their mass departure from Egypt.

I appreciate Rahab as she had come to trust this unseen God who was full of miracles and had a passion to learn of Him, whom she had never been taught. Rahab had only heard stories of the Israelites going through the Red Sea on dry ground, and what they had done to Sihon and Og, the two kings of the Amorites. Although not mentioned, I believe she may have also heard of the plagues that came upon the Egyptians many years previously. These stories and many more may have been conveyed to this harlot by merchants that passed through Jericho, or perhaps by those she entertained. Whichever way, this prostitute had a burning desire in her soul to know this unseen God and she chose to trust Him unequivocally. Rahab whose trust had already begun to grow hid the two spies that Joshua had sent in preparation for battle. We are not told in Joshua chapter 2 why these men chose her home, but it was a God ordained appointment. Rahab shared the very words with these spies that they needed to know.

Gullibly, yet with blind faith, she asked them to save her and her family when they came back to annihilate the city of Jericho. What faith this prostitute unleashed to these spies, saying –

> *... I know that the LORD has given this land to you and that a great fear of you has fallen on us, so that all who live in this country are melting in fear because of you.*
> Joshua 2:9

What a courageous faith Rahab chose to nurture – although she was a woman whom society then, and even now, would look down upon, was chosen to be in the lineage of Jesus. How gracious and merciful is our God who does not look at what the world, family, teachers, friends and culture have thrust upon us. God, with so much love, picks us up from our circumstances and gives beauty for ashes and uses us for His glory.

I want to encourage us not to look at our circumstances but at our God who uses us just as we are or where we are. Despite what we have done, or not done, He desires our heart. He wants to hear the words: "I may not be able or capable, but I give You my all, I will trust You with my future and all I encounter."

Be it imprisonment, lions, an unsavoury past, a great or difficult upbringing, culture, loving or dysfunctional parents, riches or poverty, to our God, it is irrelevant. He wants our heart our love and obedience. God will make and mould us into His image and His glory will shine.

I know of many heroes of the faith who became mighty for God and went through trials or persecution. These fires refined them, and they became like gold and precious stones for His glory. I love it that in each story shared, we are not in the trial alone, but God steps into the difficulty with us, holding us, and if we let Him, He will carry our burden. He uses ministering angels to bring love, comfort, strength, encouragement, hope or whatever is needed as He did to Jesus in the garden of Gethsemane. Ask God to grant you eyes to see your angels as they come to minister in many diverse ways in your situations.

I want to encourage each one to see ourselves as our wonderful God sees us and I pray that the verse below will lift you to heights so you can sit and rule with Him — Our wonderful God has chosen us, set us apart, transformed us, died for us and made us into His likeness.

But you are a chosen people, a royal priesthood, a holy nation, a people belonging to God, that you may declare the praises of him who called you out of darkness into his wonderful light.
1 Peter 2-9

Epilogue

My book may be complete, but not God's love, wondrous ways, or faithful promises, they will never come to an end. Visualise Jesus standing up, leaning in, listening to your heart-felt prayers, desiring to respond with power ready to unleash in your circumstances, as you truly trust Him.

I wrote much about my family, and still today they are all walking powerfully in God. Kylie has an incredible ministry with children both in the church and schools alike. Darren a Pastor and counsellor in a Pentecostal Church on Vancouver Island, Canada, Peter an amazing godly entrepreneur in the business world and ministers much in his church.

To this day, one of my greatest outings each week is to go beside the water with friends just as the sun rises and the crisp air hugs our bodies praying that the mighty power of God will be loosed in what we share with Him. Be it my personal life, present-day situations, COVID pandemic, world unrest, Jesus listens and hands each prayer to His Father interceding on my behalf.

Oh, the joy of seeing the miraculous continue to come even as I completed my last chapter. Courageously and boldly, just a couple of months ago I asked the leaders of our Life Group to pray and stand with me on James 5:14-15 praying over one of the ladies. We took this passage literally and saw a blockage in her heart totally cleared. No stent or open-heart surgery needing to be performed, much to the amazement and awe of her Brisbane Cardiologist. Melanoma cancer has been healed, accelerated and supernatural healings are becoming a natural occurrence, mental health calmed. A marriage restored after it was as dead as Lazarus, families restored now with love abounding, and so much more. The power of standing on God's promises is as real today as it was in the days of Jesus.

I could share so much more, but this is to say our God is able, our God is real, our God continues to respond to audacious faith-filled prayers as we His people trust in His mighty power.

As you experience your faith rise, you will shout out loud.
`NOTHING IS IMPOSSIBLE FOR GOD'
Your trust in Him will be unleashed as you
hold onto all God has promised.
Joy and tears will flow as answers to your prayers
you thought impossible, become a reality.

References

[1] Crouch, A. (1990). Through it All [Recorded by A. Crouch].

[2] Janner, G. (1984, July 25). Bedendox. Hansard, Vol. 64. Retrieved from UK Parliament: https://api.parliment.uk/historic-hansard/commons/1984/jul/25/debendox

[3] Harron, D. W., Grriffiths, K. & Shanks, R. G. (1980, November 22). Debendox and congenital malformations in Northern Ireland. Br Med J, Vol. 281, 1379. doi:http//doi.org/10.1136/281.6252.1379

[4] Forged, H. (1981). I will Praise You in all my Ways. In Scripture in Song, Songs of the Kingdom, Volume Two. Benson Company.

[5] Redman, M. (2013). Mercy [Recorded by M. Redman]. On Your Grace Finds Me [Album]. N. Nockels.

[6] Prince, J. (2007). Destined to Reign. Singapore: 22 Media Pte. Ltd. (page 71)

[7] Spafford, H. (1873). It Is Well with My Soul.

Printed in Australia
AUHW020602190522
363834AU00002B/2

9 781922 722638